CAGNEY BY CAGNEY

CAGNEY BY CAGNEY

James Cagney

DOUBLEDAY & COMPANY, INC.
GARDEN CITY, NEW YORK
1976

CREDITS

The Granger Collection—5, 6, 8, 9, 15, 16, 19
Tom Kelley—13
From the Homer Dickens Still Collection—14, 23
Photo by Madison Lacy—18
Photo by Mac Julian—21
Photo by Zinn Arthur—22
Wide World Photos—26
Black Star/Joe Covello—27, 28, 29, 30
Roger Marshutz—31, 32
Photograph by Floyd McCarty—33
Sports Illustrated photo by Roy DeCarava © Time, Inc.—34

DESIGNED BY LAURENCE ALEXANDER

Library of Congress Cataloging in Publication Data

Cagney, James, 1899–
    Cagney by Cagney.

    1. Cagney, James, 1899–   I. Title.
PN2287.C23A33   791.43′028′0924 [B]
        ISBN: 0-385-04587-5
Library of Congress Catalogue Card Number: 74-18784
Copyright © 1976 by Doubleday & Company, Inc.

To

FRANCES VERNON CAGNEY

and

CAROLYN NELSON CAGNEY

two gals who deserve the palm

My thanks to John McCabe and Jack Thomas
for helping me remember it all

Each man starts with his very first breath
To devise shrewd means for outwitting death.

CAGNEY BY CAGNEY

CAGNEY BY CAGNEY. How's that for a fatheaded title? I use it as kind of an official scorecard because I don't seem to own my own name. Three biographies so far. First: *Cagney*. Second: *James Cagney*. Third: don't remember, but Cagney's sure in the title. What I have read from these is heavy with cockeyed conclusions and some solid misinformation. What I now propose to give you will at least come from someone who knows Cagney pretty well.

An old friend, Ralph Wheelwright, advised me in 1955 to get at an autobiography. Having read some show business autobiographies, I saw no reason to add to the pile of what I've always called "junk writing." But Ralph was so right when he said, "Somebody else is going to do the job if you don't—and you won't like it." I hear, moreover, there are two other Cagney books in the making. So—before any more spring up—for what they are worth, here are some reminiscences that might add up to a book.

1

Being born at the turn of this century in New York City had its hazards. The infant mortality then, particularly in the Lower East Side, was high—roughly two and a half times today's. For a time there, it looked as if I was going to be part of those statistics.

I was a very sick infant. My mother, only twenty—a mere child herself—was terribly worried, of course. What bothered her most, next to my possible demise, was the fact that I hadn't been baptized. As a good Catholic, she felt that if I were to die before I was given a proper name, I'd never be allowed into Heaven. She bemoaned this again and again to her brother: "He hasn't got a name—he has to have a name!" Now, my uncle was a pretty rough Irishman. He humored her for a while, but Mom continued to cry the house down about my lack of identity. Finally he turned on her and said, "Carrie, for God's sake, shut up! Stop your crying and call the kid 'Ikey'!"

Ikey Cagney. Sounds promising. It would have been good for a lot of laughs later.

Without hesitating I can say my mother was the key to the Cagneys. She was born Carolyn Nelson on New York's Lower East Side when poverty ruled there. She was forced to leave school at twelve. It was time to go out and get a job to help her family. When she told this to her teacher, the lady pleaded with her, "Oh, Carrie, don't leave. You've got to stay. You're the most promising pupil I have." Then the teacher just sat there, weeping silently. That was a picture my mother never forgot.

But there was no way out of it. That skinny little red-haired girl had to work in a factory, the Eagle Pencil Company, but as her days went by, one thought kept recurring until it became an obsession: I am damned well going to see to it that every kid of mine gets an education. It was a promise she kept repeating to herself the six years she worked in that factory. It was a promise she kept.

She was an attractive woman, Mom. Her red hair was the truest titian, an iridescent tint, and in the sunlight I could see brilliant yellows and purples and bright reds in it. In all my life I have never seen anyone with such hair, and it went a foot below her waist. If I may say so, it was a glory. Little wonder she attracted my dad.

The Nelsons and the Cagneys were both Lower East Side New York. My mother's mother was Irish, born in County Leitrim around 1846. She married my grandfather Nelson, an ex-sailor who ultimately graduated to the status of barge captain.

My dad's people I never knew. Dad was a man of great and easy charm and gentle—James Francis Cagney, handsome, a ladies' man. My mother would occasionally drop hints that he had never stopped being a ladies' man. He was five foot eight—built like all us kids—stocky, but quick and graceful on his feet. A very good boxer, an excellent ballplayer. "Jimmy Steam" they called him because of his fast ball. I'll never forget the time many years later when we all first saw Jackie Gleason. We were stunned. Jackie's style, approach, mannerisms—everything—was my dad to the life.

When Mom and Pop began their married life it was in the neighborhood near Avenue D and Eighth Street on the Lower East Side. There my brother Harry was born in 1898, and I came a year later, July 17, 1899. When I was two, we moved to 429 East Seventy-ninth Street, a better neighborhood, and not long after, we went to 166 East Ninety-sixth Street. All this while, young Cagneys kept coming along. There was Eddie, born in 1902, and Bill in 1904. The following year little Gracie joined us, but she died of pneumonia at ten weeks of age. In 1916, my last brother, Robert, was born. As a late child, of course, we were crazy about him, but he developed tubercular meningitis and died at thirteen months. The best was inevitably saved for last: my sister Jeanne, who came along when her four brothers were young men, which meant four fathers, my father having died the previous November.

My first vivid recollections of New York were of Seventyninth Street, a wide thoroughfare lined with brownstone-front houses, all built into flats for the steady, sensible working people who lived in our neighborhood. It was only in 1912 or so when the neighborhood began to sour under the infiltration of the scabrous dope pushers who came in.

As a youngster, of course, I was very much a city boy, but one day my dad rented an open four-wheeler known as a barouche and piled me, my mother, and three brothers into it for a two-week visit to my great-aunt in the then open country that is now Flatbush. That vivid memory is with me yet, and I can still see the tremendous elm in her front yard and the morning glories growing on the white picket fence. Ever since those two glorious weeks at the turn of the century, morning glories have been my favorite flower and, just as lasting in its effect, during those few days I changed from a city boy to a country boy. When I returned to Seventy-ninth Street from Flatbush after two weeks of freedom in the golden air, I was indescribably saddened. It is enough to say that I have loved the country ever since, totally.

Not that life on Seventy-ninth Street was dull. In 1904–5, some houses were being built across the street from us one winter, and the night watchman hired to protect the building materials sat close to his stove in his little shack in front of the construction site. Some neighborhood kids decided to liven things up by peeing down his stovepipe, and the resulting odor drove the man out in a fury to catch the wrongdoers. The one he caught and frantically beat up was my brother Harry, who was purely a bystander. My mother at the time possessed two handy items: a thick, six-foot-long horsewhip and a blazing temper. When she heard of the injustice done to Harry, she put on her little jacket, ran downstairs to the watchman, and whipped him up and down the street. He howled his head off, but he never bothered Harry again.

Another time, my little brother Ed, in colliding with a dog, had hurt his head badly on the pavement and thereafter was subject to episodes of severe brain inflammation. One day when he was in school just recovering from a siege of meningitis, he made the mistake of whispering to the boy next to him. A teacher walking down the aisle heard Ed whisper. So this instructor reached down, grabbed Ed by the hair, yanked him out of his seat, and beat both sides of that sensitive little head. Ed ran home crying and when my mother heard the story, she put on her little jacket again, and went out looking for the teacher. The brave fellow was hiding and remained in hiding for days after. He knew Carolyn Cagney was looking for him.

My father's temperament was slightly less feisty. After working for a time as a bookkeeper, he obliged a bartender friend of his who couldn't show up for work one evening by taking his place behind the bar. This was no hardship for Pop. From early on he had been rather well acquainted with saloons. He knew how to serve the product, and he knew how to consume it. So attractive indeed was this life that later on he bought his own saloon.

One of my earliest memories is of the first day I ever entered school at the age of six when I went very proudly into Pop's saloon and told him that I had learned a song. He gave me a glass of sarsaparilla, set me up on the bar, and told me to go ahead. Whereupon I belted out this minor classic:

> Fly away, fly away, birdee-o, dadadada.
> Bring her a feather and bring her a song—
> And that will please birdee-o all the day long.

We were a musical family, the piano always on the go, and all of us invariably fooling around with a tune. I used to sing "I Want a Girl—Just Like the Girl Who Married Dear Old Dad" for my mother and father, and they'd sit there, holding hands, beaming like the summer sun.

Pop's gentle waywardness was thoroughly engrained. He had the charm of an Irish minstrel, he did everything to the tune of laughter—but he was totally deficient in a sense of responsibility to his family. Despite this, he always thought he was doing well for us. At times, things got very rough. At best he had a spotty job record: here a job, there a job, and long stretches of nothing in between. This coincided with the Cagney boys all trying to get through college and working after school, so that at times it was only our part-time jobs that put the groceries on the table.

Still—though we were poor, we didn't *know* we were poor. We realized we didn't get three squares on the table every day, and there was no such thing as a good second suit, but we had no objective knowledge that we were poor. We just went from day to day doing the best we could, hoping to get through the really rough periods with a minimum of hunger and want. We simply didn't have time to realize we were poor, although we did realize the desperation of life around us. I recall the Fitzpatrick family on Ninety-sixth Street who were put out on the sidewalk when they couldn't pay the rent, and this not long after they had seen their little child run over by a refuse wagon. The Cagneys never had that kind of experience, thank God, and it never occurred to us, despite the poverty, to hold our heads or feel sorry for ourselves. We just did the best we could.

Another of Pop's little weaknesses was the horses. After he died, my mother found an old checkbook among his effects, and the stubs read as high as $150 and $200, all to his bookmaker. That money would have seemed a fortune to us if we had seen even half of it.

But he was irrepressible. He sailed happily through life, charming everyone, and all the time belting down the sauce that I suppose helped to sustain both his charm and his improvidence. When the flu epidemic of 1918 came along, the inroads of all that booze made him an easy victim. Dead in two swift, terrible days. My mother loved him deeply, and his going was an agony for her. But despite the terrible loss she felt after Pop left, despite the aching sorrow she knew seeing her man die before her eyes, she was staunch stuff. This sturdy lady kept the family intact, and we boys worked to help keep us all together.

The family was always very tightly knit. Harry, my oldest

brother, was a flawless athlete—trackman, a crack swimmer, a magnificent diver. Like all of us, he made almost a religion of never giving up. Once when the family was in its usual financial straits—deep, stony broke—Harry entered the 71st Regiment Collegiate track meet. We were so poor that he couldn't afford to buy sneakers, so he borrowed a pair of ordinary rubbers, lashed them to his feet—and won. He was only about twelve when he decided to become a doctor, despite all the financial hurdles he had to face. The thing that triggered this decision was seeing my mother in Presbyterian Hospital suffering from the effects of a gall bladder operation.

Harry entered medical school at Columbia, and in the summer of 1918 he was forced to take time out for a hernia operation. At that very same time he was on the Columbia diving team. He had the hernia operation, and immediately after entered the diving competitions. The coach and the doctor okayed it on the proviso that Harry wear a tightly taped bandage; so, swathed in that restrictive binding, Harry went right ahead and won the intercollegiate fancy diving championship.

I can remember, when I was in high school, Harry getting up at night, walking the floor until three in the morning, pounding his studies into his head, boning up for his exams. In the middle of med school, the financial hardships made him drop out, and one of his professors told him sadly that this would be the end of it. Med school dropouts, he said, never came back. Harry denied that, said he'd be back the following year. He was, and he got a medical degree in 1925.

Not that Harry was a humorless grind. He had a great sense of mischief, always teasing, and one day he kidded a beautiful girl in our neighborhood, who reported it to her brother. The brother came charging out to find Harry and me on the curbstone. Bup (that was the brother's very stimulating name) stopped and said to his sister, "Them?" "Yes." "What the hell! Do you think I want to get killed?," and he charged right back into the house. That will indicate to some extent the Cagney brothers' reputation.

Harry was a great athlete, bigger and stronger than I, but he couldn't fight worth a damn. Anytime he was in trouble he announced to the opposition that he had a brother who could lick anyone. I was elected to do the fighting, and I didn't mind it a bit. I did the same thing for my brother Ed, but my brother Bill was a very feisty, gutsy little guy who could "go" when necessary. His perennial enemy, about a head taller than he, was Eddie Kinlan, and those two were always ready (as we said in those days) to "hook it up." One day when they really went at it, it proved a standoff because someone stopped the fight. Bill came home and complained to my mother that someone had broken up their fight. Mom asked him if he had been losing. "No." Had he been winning? "No." Mom, in her wisdom knowing that it would have to be settled sometime, told Bill to go out and find Eddie and have it out. "Then when you do," she said, "I'll make you the best dinner you ever had." Bill promptly went around the corner to the Kinlans' place, knocked on the door, and when Eddie's dad answered, said to him, "I'm Willie Cagney. I want Eddie to come and fight it out with me."

Mr. Kinlan beamed, turned back to his son somewhere in the house and said, "Ah, *hah*. All right, Eddie, come and fight it out." Bill couldn't see Eddie, who was deep in the house, but he could see the expression on Mr. Kinlan's face as he watched his boy's reaction. Clearly Eddie was dogging it, wanted no part of Bill, and in obvious frustration the old man yelled at Bill, "Get outta here, you little bastard, or I'll break your leg." So Bill left, reported all this to my mother, and she said, "Fine, son!," giving him a dinner he was very happy to consume.

I think this story illustrates as well as any the kind of neighborhood we were raised in. My mother, having been brought up on the Lower East Side where fighting was a part of life's everyday fabric, knew that this was the way it was, and running away did no one any good.

Ed never fought, however. He was a gentle lad. But as I say, there certainly was genuine athletic accomplishment in the family. Ed became a powerful wrestler and All-Scholastic soccer center; Harry, in addition to his diving, was a good ballplayer.

Harry once had an argument with a good street fighter nicknamed Bulldog. Harry boasted to Bulldog that he had a brother who could lick him, and I duly did just that. Some weeks later, Bulldog courageously challenged me again, and in making our arrangements, he uttered this deathless line, "Nobody's gonna get tough over me no more." Again, Bulldog was put away.

Around this time my brother Ed, just up out of a sickbed, had been badly beaten up by a local boy, Willie Carney. Carney having tried to steal a golf ball Ed was playing with. I went looking for Carney but couldn't find him. That night a kid came up to our flat breathlessly to announce that Carney was fighting with a kid down the block. I arrived in time to see the kid stretched out, and I promptly told the boy I'd take his place. I gave Carney a chance to rest, and then we went to it. We were going at it hot and heavy when the cops arrived and broke it up. By arrangement we met the next night and were slugging away when the cops raided that one, too. The third night we kept slugging away, but he just refused to fold. I had great admiration for that spunky guy because he took my best punches with style. Once I feinted with my left and hit him a stiff right on the chin that should have finished him, but he just rubbed his chin with the back of his hand and kept right on coming.

As for me, my shirtfront was covered with blood—his blood. Nothing could stop Carney. There was a crowd around us, twelve deep, and one compassionate little Jewish lady kept saying, "These boys are killing each other. Where are their mothers? Why don't their mothers come and stop all this bloodshed?" Interestingly, my mother *was* there—right in the front ranks, watching her boy take care of things. Carney kept punching and so did I until I broke my hand on him, and we agreed that, once mended, we'd finish the fight. I was in splints the next six weeks, but by the end of that time, Carney was in reform school.

When I went up to the hospital to have my hand set, the doctor complimented me on the beautiful colors in the black eye Carney had laid on me, and he asked me how the hand had been broken. I said, "Well, I was riding my bike, a truck came along, and in swerving to get out of the way, the bike fell. The handle-bar hit my eye, and my fist crashed into the curbstone." The doc said very dryly, "Really? And what does the other guy look like?" The other guy didn't look too bad. I never met him again, but I was to hear from Carney later in life, a story I'll come to in due time.

There was almost a kind of chivalry about street fighting in our neighborhood. If two fellas were fighting (incidentally, I always say "fella"; pronouncing it as a rhyme to "mellow" would strike me as slightly overdone), as I say, if two fellas were fighting on our street, and one fella was getting badly beaten, he could nominate someone to take his place. One little guy, Peewee, was fighting a left-hander who could really punch, and Peewee sud-denly got a powerhouse belt on the eye. It was a swift punch, so swift that none of us watching could see that it had been deliv-ered by the other fighter's older brother, standing on the sidelines. But when Peewee hit the sidewalk, he pointed to the real culprit and said, "*He* hit me!"

The culprit, a big kid about seventeen, said he hadn't. With that, I stepped in to take Peewee's place—and got clobbered im-mediately. I didn't see the brother's punch coming either, and I wound up with a shiner the color of Joseph's coat and found the fight was stopped. Sometimes it doesn't pay to be chivalrous.

My mother's dad, Grandpa Nelson, was a rough and excit-able sailor who had attained his barge captaincy in the years when I knew him. I loved him and my grandmother very much, and I used to visit them during trips from port to port as a tug pulled their loads of lumber and coal. I can still recall the fresh doughnuts and milk Grandmother served in that cozy little cabin. Grandpa was a scrapper, and invariably when he had his *own* load on in some saloon or other, he was "on the prod." Unfailingly he would get the hell knocked out of him. A guy would belt him across the room to the other wall, and Grandpa would pick him-self up carefully and say menacingly to his assailant, "Have you had enough?" He never grew too old to take a poke from any-body.

Years later when I was in the picture business, I met a captain of Royal Norwegian Air Force Intelligence who knew firsthand the Norwegian town in which my grandfather, Henry Nelson, was born. "Henry Nelson—of Dröbak?" said the captain. "Impossible. There are no Nelsons in Dröbak, never have been." I then conjectured to the captain that in view of my grandfather's notorious temper, he may have done something calamitous when in his cups, a something that forced him to change his name to Nelson. I also told the captain that Grandpa had tattooed on his burly, clawlike hands the initials "A. S." "Ah, now," said the captain, "that could well be Samuelson, because Dröbak is full of Samuelsons." Which is as good a guess as any about my grandfather's origins and early history.

He and Grandmother came to live with us in 1907, and she died three years later. He lived on to the age of seventy-two, and when he died in 1912 after a broken hip led to pneumonia, he still owned a full head of healthy brown hair.

My childhood was surrounded by trouble, illness, and my dad's alcoholism, but as I said, we just didn't have time to be impressed by all those misfortunes. I have an idea that the Irish possess a built-in don't-give-a-damn that helps them through all stress. Moreover, we had the advantage of an awful lot of love in our family, and wherever I lived when I was a kid—East Seventy-ninth Street, East Ninety-sixth Street, Ridgewood out on Long Island, and back again to Manhattan—we had each other, and that was enough. We went to church every Sunday and instructions every Tuesday to become good Catholics. We all made our First Holy Communion and received Confirmation at the proper time. Harry was even an altar boy for a while.

If we didn't have much in material gain, we were amply supplied with the best in nonmaterial gain—lots of laughs. Brother Ed was the wit of the family, and probably for that and for his youth, he was the favorite among the brothers. His humor never diminished. When he was seven we were living in Ridgewood in somewhat cramped quarters. Ed and Harry slept in my mother's very large bedroom; Harry and I slept together in a bed at the end of the room. Bedtime was eight o'clock, which was also the time for Harry and me to knock hell out of each other. One night we were at it, and Mom ordered us to stop. We didn't, and in the dark we could hear her scrambling for her shoes at the side of the bed. "Boys, if you don't stop," she said, "I'm going to let this shoe fly at you." Then up piped little Eddie in his reedy voice to chant a popular song of the day, "Shoo, fly, don't bother me; shoo, fly, don't bother me." That broke us up for fair.

When Eddie grew up to be a doctor, that wit was always with him. Another doctor who went through med school with Ed was a congenital sourpuss, having no time for humor or life's little pleasantries. Some years after graduation, Ed was talking with some of his classmates and the name of this uncongenial friend came up. "Whatever happened to him?" one doctor asked. Someone replied that he had become a proctologist. Ed immediately shot back, "Mirror, mirror, on the wall!"

Bill was always the businessman of the family and showed a distinct salesman's flair from very early age. When he was eight, a cauliflower peddler showed up on our street. He stopped at the corner, put the weight on his horse's bit, and called all the street youngsters around him. "Listen, kids," he said, "you go up through that apartment house and see how many of these cauliflowers you can sell. For every one you sell, I'll give you two cents apiece." Bill, who weighed fifty pounds at most, took a big bag of the vegetables, climbed up five flights, and started to hawk them from door to door. He sold all he had, came down to get another bag, and went right back up to sell some more. It is the simple truth that Bill was born shrewd, and thenceforth was always on the prowl for a good deal.

Once he was selling advertising for a women's wear magazine, and on his lunch hour he'd go to a nearby auction room to pick up bargains and sell them at a nice profit. This was instinctive, as was his flair for gambling. As a superb poker player and knight errant of the pool table, he would have been a kingpin among professional gamblers if he had ever taken that route. Even during high school he was making extra money at the pool

1. Assertive even in the cradle, 1899.

2. Carolyn Nelson, First Holy Communion.

3. Carolyn Nelson. The hair was curly, red, *and* beautiful.

4. The ball team of the famous Nut Club, Yorkville. Catcher Cagney in the last row, second from left.

5. The scene that made grapefruit famous. Mae Clarke on the receiving end. *The Public Enemy,* 1931.

6. With Jean Harlow. *The Public Enemy.*

tables at lunch hour, and after school, it was over to the friendly neighborhood crap game. Inevitably he became a salesman, and top-flight, too. When I was out in Hollywood and in need of someone to do the business end for me, I asked Bill to come out. That worked out very well indeed. Bill's business acumen over the years has been notable, and to this day I go to him for counsel on such matters because my judgment in this area I trust not a damn.

When Bill and I were youngsters, I had the sweet tooth of the family, but he was close runner-up. One time when he was ill, he was given pennies by my mother to make him feel a little better. In those days, some stores sold broken chips of Nabisco cream crackers at a penny a bag. Quite a bargain. Bill got a sack of these chips with one of his pennies, and my sweet tooth set me quivering on his trail, hounding him down for some of them. I followed Bill until I found a way to get those chips for free. The way was simple, and it brought out the ham in me for the first time. I pretended I was a monkey, scratching my sides, making idiot faces and grunting, "Feed the monkey! Feed the monkey!" This amused him considerably and he kept pushing the Nabiscos at me. The realization that he had given all his sweets away made him go into his howling act. The wail immediately brought my mother. She cuffed me as I deserved and got Bill some more crackers. I didn't realize until much later that this was my first paid acting job.

Another time Bill got an apple and I asked him for a bite. He offered it to me surrounded by as much of his hands as could cover the apple. I took him by both wrists so he wouldn't escape, and I bit into that apple like a little crocodile. When I pulled away, three quarters of it was in my mouth, and Bill did the banshee again. The louder he screamed, the faster I chewed.

I was good in school, particularly in spelling. When we moved to Ridgewood I can remember it was no trouble winning the monthly dollar Mom used to give the one who had the best report card. It was also in Ridgewood that I had a spectacular spelling bee victory. After I had spelled everybody else down, the teacher kept feeding me words for another half hour, and it was plainly boring her. Then came the word "sovereign," and I blew it. The look of blessed relief on her face is with me yet.

But Ridgewood was too good to last. We moved back to the hurly-burly of East Seventy-ninth Street, and that was saddening. I went from straight A's on my report card to B's and C's. In time, those feelings were raised a bit by my first encounter with the ladies. My first love (I was five) was a girl named Annie. I never knew her last name. She was probably ten or twelve, and used to come by my house on her way to and from school. Whether by accident or design, my shoelaces were always untied when Annie strolled by, and her sense of neatness drove her to stop and tie them. My next love was a beautifully delicate American girl, and I designate her nationality because our area was almost exclusively first-generation German, Irish, Jewish, Italian, Hungarian, and Czech.

This "pure American" girl was the sister of a friend of mine, and I simply worshiped her beauty from afar, never once speaking to her. Years later I met the chap who married her, and I learned to my very real sorrow that she had died in her twenties.

The polyglot nature of my neighborhood is the basic reason why all my life I've had such an appreciation and understanding of dialects. I ought to—I was surrounded by them. Indeed, I was twenty-two before I ever met an elderly man who spoke without an accent, and when I heard this fella speak, I was actually startled. We kids picked up all kinds of phrases from the Italians, the Czechs, the Germans, and the Jews, and in school I was a rather good German student. At least 90 per cent of my classmates were Jewish, mostly up from the Lower East Side, and as I studied German, I learned the Yiddish equivalent from my Jewish pals. I still speak some German but a lot more Yiddish.

Many popular songs of my youth were parodied in Yiddish by clever music hall comedians. Years later, my friend Noel Madison, who perennially acted gangsters in Hollywood movies, taught me a sprightly Yiddish version of "Alice Blue Gown" that I still fondly remember:

In my little *baysaschmidrush* downtown,
When I first put my new *tallis* on,
I was both proud and shy.
Als ruv passed me by; he wished me *gut Yontiff;*
Ich hob gezugt alivai.
Then the rabbeh gave me an *aliyah,*
Oh, she whispered right into my ear:
"How much can you *schnorrer?*"
Ich hob gezugt, "Please don't bother—
In my little *baysaschmidrush* downtown."

Translated, this goes approximately:

In my little temple downtown,
When I first put my new prayer shawl on,
I was both proud and shy.
As the old rabbi passed me by; he wished me good holiday;
I said it should happen to me.
Then the rabbi's wife gave me quite an honor;
Oh, she whispered right into my ear:
"How much can you contribute?"
I said, "Please don't bother—
In my little temple downtown."

I enjoy speaking Yiddish. It's a wonderful tongue for story-telling, and on occasion I've inserted a few bits of Yiddish dialogue in the pictures for the sure-fire comedy effect. We realized when we did it that there would be very little small-town reaction, but in the big towns where there was a substantial Jewish population the effect was pretty stimulating.

Our neighborhood gloried in exotic types. There was, for example, my friend Maud. Of the girls in our age group, she could fight better than anyone else, so she became their leader. She was a lefty, and when I boxed with her (always without boxing gloves, of course), she would absolutely stiffen me with that left. Her stomach punch would carry through to my backbone. What were my fists doing all this time? Sparring, of course. It wouldn't be gentlemanly to actually *hit* a girl, even one a foot taller.

I remember once a little blocky girl, leader of the Seventy-seventh Street girls, tossed a challenge at my girl, and a match was arranged. With the wild cheers of each gang ringing in their ears, the two girls commenced to beat hell out of each other. Queensbury rules—no hair pulling or face scratching.

A dope addict ("cokie" or "hophead" we called them then) named Daly was urging the little blocky girl on very loudly. Fat Bella, one of Maud's pals, said a few words to him, he replied in kind to her, and she retorted with an overhand right. Daly grabbed the wide, tightly wired ribbon in her hair and swung her off her feet, making her go round and round like a Roman candle. Then we young kids jumped Daly and heaved rocks at him as he scuttled up the street. Maud's fight flowered into another between two younger girls about ten years old. The brother of one of the girls stepped in, slapped his sister in the face, and told her to go home. Then this little child said indignantly to her brother, "Well, she ain't gonna call *me* no whore!"

People. Wonderful, remarkable people. This, it seems to me, is what an autobiography should be rich in—the people who make up a person's real environment. For the past fifteen years I have grumbled my reasons to various people why I have refused all along to do an autobiography. One time in reply to a pal who suggested I put it all down, I versified

> Mine not the searching eye;
> Mine not to ask the why;
> Mine not to vie with wit;
> Mine not to give a damn.

There are ladies present.

But, on reflection, in addition to setting the record straight about my life, I have come to realize that these pages give me the chance to talk about these wonderful people who have enriched my life, and I propose to do so. A particular friend of mine has tagged me "the faraway fella" for reasons that I'll presently uncover. On the whole it seems an appropriate designation and a fitting subtitle for all I set down here, but an equally appropriate subtitle would be *The Remarkable People.* People fascinate the hell out of me. Frankly, most biographies and autobiographies bore me witless because things the authors find engrossing, I frequently don't. I'll put the onus on myself there. What is trivia to me is undoubtedly very important to the writer and I don't want to second guess him. But the fact remains that in a number of show business autobiographies, for example, I find (for my taste) too much of the author's connections with the upper reaches of society and not nearly enough of the really remarkable people who make up his workaday world.

One of the most remarkable people in my life is Artie Klein, my second oldest living friend. (Pete Snyder is the oldest.) Like most of my closest pals in the early days, Artie was Jewish, coming along when I was about thirteen. I first met Artie on the dock when I "hooked it up" with "The Jap." The Jap was a lefty, and he threw that hand into my belly until I damned near threw up. Finally, in a clinch, I coughed as a preliminary to vomiting, and that seemed to clear my head, giving me my second wind. I worked the boy over and beat him rather badly.

The Jap was Jewish but had slanting eyes and looked decidedly oriental, hence the nickname. Nicknames proliferated along our street. If a kid was dark-skinned, Caucasian or not, he became "Yellow" or "Nigger." A very light-haired fella was "Whitey"; a diminutive boy was "Shorty," and a guy needing a haircut was "Wiggy." The fella running errands for the drugstore had to be "Doc." One lad when asked what was the matter with so-and-so answered, "Oh, he's got a skinthease!," meaning skin disease. He was called "Skinthy" from then on, even into adulthood. I was always "Red" because my hair was the solidest of that hue in our family.

But back to Artie. Artie was always Artie, and so he is to this day. I still call him about every week, and we go over the old days. He was with me when I had some of my most memorable "hook ups." Once as he, a pal named Bert, and I were walking down First Avenue, a couple of characters on the corner of Eighty-seventh Street were watching as we strolled by. Suddenly one of these lads started for Bert and he took off down the street. It seemed the pursuing guy's gal friend rather fancied Bert. I looked at one of the remaining characters, and it was clear he was spoiling for a fight. "Looking for trouble?" I said. He replied with a beautiful right that caught me over the left eye.

My head flipped back and I saw a spectacular flash of yellow light, but through it all I heard Artie say, "Go ahead, Red!" He caught the new hat I was wearing before it hit the ground. I was glad he made the catch as that hat had cost me $1.50 just the day before. As to the size of the gent I was facing, I was standing on the curbstone, a foot high, and I was looking right into his Adam's apple. We went at it. He threw some of those long roundhousers, hoping to nail me again, but I stepped inside and threw a short right to the nose. I heard it break. And this big clown who had just (to use a word then current) "sundayed" me, broke into tears, and in answer to my "Had enough?" agreed sobbingly that he had.

Artie was always there for some of my roughest moments, and I'll go ahead of my story a bit to those desperate years in vaudeville when my wife and I were abjectly, stony broke. On a crosstown bus, who should sit down beside me but Artie. We were so glad to see each other that he changed his plans for the evening and spent it with us in our shabby apartment. He asked if things were rough, and I said they were rougher than that. In answer to another direct question I said, "Yes, I *could* use some money," at which he took out his wallet and gave me half his weekly salary. The salary was sixteen bucks a week. At the time he was a Wall Street board boy, the one who chalks up the quotations, then erases them as the changes occur. That eight dollars looked like big money to us, as indeed it was. Every week thereafter for some weeks Artie would show up with eight bucks, half his substance. Not long after, I got a job and sent him a check for the total amount, but he sent it back. I argued with him, pointing out that I had only borrowed the money, but Artie is Hungarian, and the stubbornness of Hungarians is legendary. He would never take that money back, and it was only much later that we were in a position to return his warm good will by having him and his wife as guests at our farm for many summers. You don't forget rare ones like Artie Klein.

Nor another friend in that category, a fella who has been close to me for well over fifty years—Jim Fair. He, his wife, and I have been friends all that time. Before the Hollywood days when my wife and I were out in California visiting my mother-in-law, we were comparatively affluent, with a season of vaudeville behind us. But we stayed just a little too long and found ourselves strapped financially. In order to get back to New York we had to reach our only acquaintance then who was really solvent—Jim Fair—he having worked many years at a good salary for the New York *Times*.

I sent Jim a wire, and the money came to us immediately. On our way across the country, we got off in Chicago, and I dropped into the Chicago *Tribune* office where a friend was working. He got on one end of the telegraph wire and reached Jim on the other end at the *Times*. The very first thing Jim asked me was, "Do you need any more of that California medicine?" Happily, we didn't, and when I got back to New York and started working again, I paid Jim, and we were in fairly good condition from then on. One of life's bounties is that the Jim Fairs and the Artie Kleins were there when we needed them, and we haven't forgotten that.

But returning to my very early years, another thing I've never forgotten is when I was about twelve and my education-conscious mother took me to a lecture on what is now called ecology. It was termed conservation then, and my realizing for the first time that land erosion was an actual living threat to our world was a shock I've never really gotten over. This, together with my fervent and unchanging love of the countryside, made me think seriously for a while of becoming a forester or scientific agriculturist. But although I followed neither of these professions, their urgencies and deep concerns are mine and have been mine throughout my life.

I almost can't remember a time when I wasn't working. My first regular job was at fourteen when I got up daily at five-thirty to make my breakfast and go down to Park Row and the old New York *Sun,* where I was an office boy. I delivered proofs and copies of the newspaper to uptown firms, and off I'd go, all ninety-seven pounds of me, with a heavy roll of newspapers under one arm and a mountainous load of advertising proofs under the other. Off to all the big stores—Bloomingdale's, Stern's, Altman's, Bonwit Teller's—and each one got their set of proofs and papers. I was carrying a load that seemed to weigh more than I did, and my reward once a week was a packet containing five bucks, which I handed to my mother unopened. That was, as I say, my first regular job, but before that I had been selling programs in the armories, and for this I got fifty cents an evening. That first fifty-cent piece I handed my mother made us both glow with pride.

An after-school job was mandatory for us boys. We couldn't have subsisted otherwise. By the time I was fifteen, the three oldest boys—Harry, Eddie, and I—were working at the New York Public Library. My beginning salary was twelve dollars and a half per month, for which I worked twenty-two and a half hours a week. After a year, I became a custodian at a splendid increase to seventeen and a half dollars a month. Our job was to pick up books left on the table and return them to their proper place on the shelves. On Saturdays, in the kids' section, this could be and was murderous. This at the time was my day job. At night I worked at the Lenox East Settlement House to pick up some extra bucks, and on Sunday I worked as a ticket seller on the Hudson River Day Line to pick up some *extra* extra bucks. Let's say I was busy.

All this while I was going to Stuyvesant High School, where I also picked up a little education with my fists. My street fights weren't wild scrambles. I knew how to box from the age of six, when a mature neighborhood boy showed me how to jab, feint, hook left, cross with a right, *and* a hook—the business. I used to work out with real fighters, and one pro gave me extended training in things I already knew basically.

Then I learned that a friend of mine had made ten dollars in a preliminary bout, so without saying a word to my mother, I began to train for a pro encounter. I'd get up very early before school, run a couple of miles, and come back in. With the loss of rest and a training diet that forbade sugar, I was very quickly the shape of a rail. One morning Mom took a look at me and pointedly asked about my going out so early, and what did I think I was doing to myself? I explained eagerly that I could make ten bucks easily in a preliminary because I could lick most of those fellas without strain. "Well, that's just fine," Mom said, "but can you lick me?" "No, and I'm not even going to try," I said. She explained that's what I'd have to do before I could do any professional fighting, so just at its genesis my ring career came to an end.

But the non-professional battles never seemed to stop. One night I was doing my homework and a kid rushed in to say that a marauding gang from Eighty-third Street had arrived. I ran down to the street to behold a surging broomstick fight, so I grabbed one of them out of the hands of an Eighty-third warrior and charged into battle. Big brave me, and you can spell that d-o-p-e. As I went swinging and banging right and left, out of the blackness came a brick, which caught me in the left side. I went to my knees and stayed there. I crawled to the curb, violently sick, and for years after, those lower ribs would spasm and hurt like hell.

The biggest claim to fame in our neighborhood was when you could throw a punch. Anybody who couldn't was in a bad way. To establish a reputation, to be respected by the other lads in the area, one had to take care of oneself with the fists. This is why I emphasize all the street fighting we did. The fights were simply an extreme attempt to call attention to oneself as "a hell of a fella." Need I say that this is also a pattern of history—the American Indian, the warriors of the Masai in Africa—and so many more?

In our neighborhood, we continually had to prove ourselves. My friend Bootah, for instance, hung by his fingertips from the copings of roofs five stories high to show what a brave guy he was. The boys who had no talents or little intellectual equipment took the best available shortcut to the forefront: they became prize fighters. Some of our neighborhood boys who did that had no talent at all. With no skill, just guts, they went deliberately into the fight business and became club fighters. This meant most of them wound up with cauliflower ears and noses to match. But those scars were the badges of their trade and occasion for pride. The boys had to some tangible degree proven themselves.

About all this street fighting I've discussed, it's important to remember that the Cagney kids conformed to the well-established neighborhood pattern. We weren't exceptional. We weren't battling phenomena or hyper-aggressive. We weren't anything more than normal kids reacting to our environment—an environment in which street fighting was an accepted way of life. And in reacting to that environment we had what I suppose could be called colorful young lives. Some while back I visited Ninety-sixth Street again and knocked on the door of a family who had been on the block since our years there, 1909, 1910. I identified myself to Mrs. Fisher, the mother of an early pal of mine. "Oh, yes," she said. "I remember you. You were the boy who was always fighting." I must say I was surprised at that. I never realized I was always fighting.

For much-needed recreation I played baseball with a team sporting the glamorous monicker of the Yorkville Nut Club, a title that described at least a few of its members. For much-needed income not long after I graduated from Stuyvesant High School, I got a job in an architect's office. At that time my brothers were working their way through college at Tiffin's Tea Room on 114th Street. I had three free evenings a week, so I asked my brothers if they could get me a job at Tiffin's, which they quickly did. We had a merry time of it because with all of us looking so much alike, the average customer was baffled as to the identity of his waiter. When one of us would be called, the gracious reply was, "My *brother* has your table." A very efficient arrangement—for the Cagneys.

Both 1918 and 1919 were years of great change for my family as for many others. I had been making tentative stabs at art work from the age of six, so the Student Army Training Corps at Columbia University interested me because it encouraged those who could draw to enlist in their camouflage unit. So at one fell swoop I became art student, soldier, and college boy. Because of my long-felt interest in sketching, I settled down to my studies with anticipation. One of my non-art classes was in oral reading, and I was perfectly fine in it except that my rate of speech was so rapid fire that the poor professor couldn't understand me. Very patiently he would explain the proper tempo to me, and I knew exactly what he meant. The difficulty was that when I tried it, I'd rush along with the old rat-a-tat-tat. I daresay he had adequate reason to flunk me. Also at Columbia, I was in the band as a drummer, a function I enjoyed very much. I think I was the only one in the group who couldn't read music.

I was at Columbia when my dad died. I got a message he was about to leave for the hospital, so I hurried home to accompany him, but he had gone. I took the streetcar, and when I arrived at the hospital I went to the desk nurse and said, "I want to see Mr. James Cagney." Her face fell.

"Oh, I'm sorry," she said. "He died this morning." The flu epidemic was then raging, and caskets were piled six or seven high outside the cemeteries, so many people were afflicted. Mom was carrying Jeannie at the time, and Dad was sent to the hospital so that Mom would be safe from infection. So quickly had my sunny, charming old man left us. Old! He was just forty-one.

I returned to the Army and Columbia, but with war's end and the birth of Jeannie, the need to keep the family exchequer in good shape came back as strongly as ever. As respite from my various jobs, I played a lot of baseball on Sundays with the Nut

Club, and this was an endeavor right in harmony with the times. In those days our idols weren't movie stars or ham politicians. We revered the great men of baseball, and how wonderful those names sound even now all these years after: John McGraw, Christy Mathewson, Hooks Wiltse, Larry Doyle, Fred Merkel, Roger Bresnahan, and Art Fletcher! Not long ago my wife was going through some old trunks and found the baseball uniform I wore with the Nut Club. I also managed to save my old catcher's mask; it's hanging on a nail in my dressing room today.

My favorite baseball memory is of the time when the prisoners' association at Sing Sing, the Mutual Welfare League, invited our ball team up to play. Numbered on their teams were a few ex-minor leaguers, so a game between us was not going to be Amateur Night by any means. When we arrived on the field, as catcher, I naturally began to warm up our pitcher. Then, right next to me, a voice said, "Hello, Red." We had been warned not to speak to the convicts so I pretended not to hear, but the voice continued, "What's the matter, you getting stuck up?" I looked and there was a kid who had sat next to me in school. "Bootah, how are you?" I said, and shook hands, another violation of the rules. I asked him what the rap was, and he said, "Five to ten. Shot a cop. Russell's up here on the same rap." There beside Bootah was a kid I knew named Russell, a fine-looking boy. They had nicked a cop during a stick-up and were sent up for assault.

The first inning began, and who should step up to the plate but another old neighborhood boy, "Dirty Neck" Jack Lafferty. He had been a particular chum of my dad's, and he told me how sorry he was to hear of his death. I remember my dad telling me that Lafferty at a very young age felt sure sometime somewhere he was going to kill someone. My dad told him not to be silly. Lafferty was the first saloon brawler my dad ever saw break a beer mug on the bar and carve another man's face with it. Later, Lafferty tried to steal an automobile belonging to a guy named Bull Mahoney, who came along in time to prevent the theft. Lafferty stuck a gun in Mahoney's belly and blew him wide open. So Lafferty's instinct as a youngster that he was bound to kill came sadly true, and for the Mahoney murder he was sentenced to twenty years-to-life. My old man, using some Tammany Hall connections, went to bat for Lafferty, and the sentence was reduced to fourteen years. And now here he was with my other neighborhood pals, playing baseball in Ossining.

Later in the game I went down to coach first base, and a man there said, "Hey, Red! You go down to the East Side House any more?" Another old chum, and before the game was over, I had met two more. Everybody on our team knew *somebody* there. That is proof, if proof be wanted, that our neighborhood produced something more than ex-vaudevillians. I will always remember July 21, 1927, a night some years after that Sing Sing ball game, because that was the night Jack Dempsey fought Jack Sharkey, it was the night I was playing in a Broadway show, and it was the night that Bootah died in the electric chair.

A question people have asked me through the years is why the Cagney boys didn't get involved with guns and crime the way my old Sing Sing pals did. The answer is simple: there wasn't a chance. We had a mother to answer to. If any of us got out of line, she just belted us, and belted us emphatically. We loved her profoundly, and our driving force was to do what she wanted because we knew how much it meant to her.

In Sidney Kingsley's play *Dead End*, one of the kids says to his mother, "Look, Ma, I'm dancin'," as he puts a hand on his head, the other on his behind, and cavorts around. This got a big laugh on Broadway, but not from me. It was a vital, sobering line because it reminded me that in our mother we always had somebody we could show off for. Whatever impressive things we did, we were saying in effect, "Look, Ma, I'm dancin'," hoping to be as big as the big men she thought us to be. We loved the great staunchness of her, and at times we four brothers together would impulsively put our arms around her, hold her, and hug her. She'd look at us, her nose would get red, and she'd start to cry. She just couldn't take all that love.

She had a wonderfully practical way of showing her love and concern for us. For instance, she introduced us to the Lenox Hill

Settlement House, with all its many activities and varied advantages for people young and old in the neighborhood. Typically she thought it would be good for a future doctor's speech skills if Harry joined the dramatics club at the House. This came at a time when I was working there, running the switchboard, racking pool balls, and serving as an unofficial 130-pound bouncer. Harry was duly cast in a play, but he became ill suddenly and I had to jump in for him. This was my real introduction to acting, but that was by no means the reason for my going into show business. The dramatic club wanted some scenery designed and I did that, working under the guidance of a man named Burton James. I painted the scenery, I drew dance posters, and I designed the cover for the House's magazine.

It was around this time that an interesting personality change came to me. When I was very young, I was very much the showoff—always doing the fancy things in catching a ball, for instance, and I suspect that's what made me a catcher. Catcher is a flashy position, with the chance to do all kinds of acrobatics—like catching those high foul balls, for one thing. But when I was about sixteen or seventeen I began to get shy and self-conscious. I mentioned this to Burton James at the Settlement House. I told him I wasn't sure of myself anymore, and he looked me right in the eye and said, "Well, maybe you're getting some sense." Which I think was a very sound observation.

But I didn't have much time to think about it because always, always, there was work. The need for that never stopped. I went on to Wanamaker's to wrap packages endlessly, and it was there that I met a fella who had some interest in show business. Inevitably he talked of it a great deal, and in the discussion I pointed out two things: I wanted a job that would pay some good money, and Wanamaker's was an unlikely place to get it. My friend and I talked about vaudeville acts and one of their prime attractions, dancing. I couldn't dance at all except for that marvelously intricate step, the Peabody, named I think after its inventor, a Boston cop. The Peabody is a dance virtually impossible to describe, but it is challenging to do and intriguing to watch. I had been shown its complicated maneuvers by a kid, Joe Hevron, at the Settlement House, and I had it all down quite pat. Incidentally, whenever these days I see those two very good professional dancers, George Murphy and George Burns, they insist I get up to do the Peabody. I haven't forgotten it. But in my Wanamaker days that was the only step I had mastered, and I felt very secure in it. My friend at the store told me that if I could dance a little bit, I might get a job with a vaudeville act then up at Keith's Eighty-first Street Theatre.

I went there at once. The act was called *Every Sailor*, and its personnel was all authentic Navy. Phil Dunning, a New York showman, at the time when he was a chief petty officer had seen this act when it was entertaining Navy men at various bases. Dunning took these sailors right off the USS *George Washington* and put them in vaudeville as an aid, so he explained, to the war effort. It was a female impersonation act, I found to my great surprise. Six guys in skirts serving basically as a chorus line, and one of the "girls" was quitting. I filled the vacancy and received, of all unbelievable sums, thirty-five dollars a week. That was a mountain of money for me in those worrisome days.

And that is how I began to learn dancing—as a chorus girl. I faked it to begin with. I would stand in the entrance, catch the real dancers, and steal their steps. Thereafter, in all the dancing shows and acts I did, I learned by watching. In those days except for ballet instruction, there were few dancing schools, no place, really, where one could learn tap dancing. All we ever did was steal from each other, modify the steps to suit ourselves, and in that way develop our individual styles. Over the years I saw such great hoofers as Harland Dixon, Johnny Boyle, and Jack Donahue do their stuff, and each one of them had something I could borrow.

The *Every Sailor* act died a natural death in time, and because I knew Mom didn't really want me in something as uncertain as show business, I got a job at a brokerage house in Broad Street as a runner. I picked up comparison slips, went to the other firms that had made the deal with us, and awaited verification that a sale had been made of the stock. Back then to my office. If that sounds dull, I am here to tell you it was dull, and I hated it with a great intensity.

Then, from somewhere, I heard there was a chorus boys' casting call for the Broadway show *Pitter Patter*. This was a musical (based on *The Hottentot*, an old Willie Collier farce) that had opened at the Longacre Theatre in September 1920. I got in the show, and all this is fairly unmemorable except for two things: I went from chorus boy to specialty dancer—and in the show I met the great girl who became my wife. I can't conceive of how lucky a guy can get, but this lady and I just celebrated our fifty-fourth wedding anniversary the other day, and it's been joy all the way. I call her "Bill" because her given name is Willard. She later feminized that a bit by prefixing a Frances. Frances Willard Vernon. So in these pages when I speak of "my Bill," I mean my wife; "Bill" solus means brother Bill. My Bill and I hit it off from the beginning, but there was some time to go and some money to make before we could get married.

To show you how deep-dyed was my habit of holding more than one job, I did any number of things in the *Pitter Patter* company to make extra dough. Ernest Truex, the leading man, needed someone to take care of his clothes. For the extra, I gladly became his dresser. During the course of the road trip they fired the other seven chorus boys, and I did the specialty spot. I must say at no increase in salary. Also while on the road, I checked all the baggage, which meant climbing up in the baggage car, putting tags on everything, and moving trunks around so they would go to the appropriate hotels where the principals were staying. This put my salary up to fifty-five dollars a week, and it was needed. Financially things were very rough at home, so I sent Mom forty dollars of my weekly salary.

When the show closed, I got a job with a dancing and singing act, Midge Miller and Her Boy Friends. I was, obviously, one of the four boy friends. Midge had some talent, the boys could dance—also *some*—but in the main it was not much of an act. I then appeared in several vaudeville sketches, the most memorable being *Dot's My Boy*, in which I was a Jewish lad whose parents sat in a theatre box to watch their progeny approvingly. Then when I did my specialty dance and the applause started, my stage mama (played by Sam Jaffe's mother, by the way) would smile and say loudly, *"Dot's* my boy!" This I followed with a poem about mothers, and that, as they say, was the act. Following this exercise in slightness, I worked an act featuring Harry Ormonde, a very good English comedian, and five girls. We were booked for our break-in at the Fox's Star Theatre, 107th Street and Lexington Avenue, and that one performance was our last. Booted out. The fact is the act wasn't much, and I don't think I contributed anything significant to the proceedings.

I did specialty dancing jobs for the next few years, winding up in a vaudeville three-act that needed a replacement for one of their number. This act was Parker, Rand, and Leach, and Mr. Leach was Archie Leach, now known to history and admiring film fans like myself as Cary Grant. When he left, it became Parker, Rand, and Cagney, an act that toured for the best part of six months. Then back once more to the discouraging job hunt. Still, one learned. There I was, a kid, ham-and-egging it around New York, standing on the Forty-seventh Street corner we vaudevillians called Panic Beach, listening to all the theatrical gossip and rumors of jobs surfacing here and there. Most of the people on Panic Beach would wait for the job call that featured their particular specialty as dancer, singer, or whatever. Me, I went to them all. The result was work in a wide variety of acts even though I knew I was taking a good chance of being fired (as I was occasionally) because I had exaggerated my abilities. But each one of these little jobs built up in me not only priceless experience but also a healthy resilience to the inevitable hard times in a tough and demanding profession.

But in the midst of all that hardship of jobs gained, jobs lost, jobs deferred, jobs lousy, jobs few, there was always the wonder of my Bill. I married her in 1922, absolutely the smartest thing I ever did in the whole course of my life, and I am still crazy about this lady. When talk of doing this autobiography began, she said, "Leave me out of it." I wish I could accommodate to this very honest modesty, but leaving her out is like leaving the wick out of the candle. I am obliged by sheer facts to say that the rock-solid honesty and sterling character of this little gal made possible our going comparatively unscathed through the years when we were in dire straits. And when I say dire straits, I mean "dire" and I mean "straits." It was rough. At times no food in the larder, big holes in the shoes. When I didn't have a penny, she was out working. Life seemed just a never-ending sequence of damned dingy, badly furnished rooms with a one-burner plate.

There were many times when I was sorely tried and decided to get out of the acting business, to go out and get any kind of job that would bring in the weekly paycheck. But every time I mentioned it, my Bill told me with pleasant firmness, no. I was to do what it seemed clear my innate abilities had prepared me to do. And I'm only pleased that I've been able to make up to her in some degree the material lacks of our early life.

On one of our up-grades on the career roller coaster, my Bill and I got jobs together in a show called *Lew Fields' Ritz Girls of 1922*, which played across the country until it reached St. Louis, where the money dried up. Lew Fields was a gent who almost made a profession of owing people money, and in this instance his creditors had seized the players' salaries. We refused to go on until we got our money, and there was much confused talk until the Brothers Shubert gave the management instructions that we were to be given enough to get back to New York. That we did, and back to another weary time of making the rounds.

The following year we appeared in something called *Lew Fields' Snapshots of 1923*, which wasn't a marked improvement on its predecessor. And on and on with more vaudeville. It is vital for me to say that outside of my Bill it is vaudeville that has had the greatest single effect on my life, both as an individual and as a performer. I still think of myself essentially as a vaudevillian, as a song and dance man. The vaudevillians I knew by and large were marvelous people. Ninety per cent of them had no schooling, but they had a vivid something or other about them that absolutely riveted an audience's attention. First of all, those vaudevillians knew something that ultimately I came to understand and believe —that audiences are the ones who determine material. They buy the tickets. It's only in *their* opinion that a thing is good or bad. Vaudevillians realized that one's opinion of oneself wasn't the determinant of value in entertainment. I remember Dr. Johnson's couplet: "The drama's laws the drama's patrons give; and we who live to please, must please to live."

Vaudevillians by persistent trial and error and unremitting hard work found out how to please. When they said something, it was generally funny and *genuinely* funny. If it was a nonspeaking act, it was usually something extraordinary in the way of physical achievement. They spent years perfecting those acts so that they knew their jobs and they did their jobs without slighting either their talent or their audience. I learned much from them because I studied them all and tried to take away from each something of the skill and persistence that characterized their best work. Frequently in coming into a new theatre to rehearse, I'd work out with the acrobats. I was simply trying to learn something about all phases of the business, even though it was the dancing that principally intrigued me.

On one of those occasions when I was absolutely stony broke in the winter of 1923–24, I took a job as assistant property man with the prestigious but poor-paying Provincetown Playhouse in Greenwich Village. For three dollars a night, I swept the stage and did all the little dirty jobs required—and I was happy to get it. The company manager, a wealthy amateur down from Harvard who took his job a mite too seriously, was my supervisor. This guy was simply playing at theatre. One night when the subways ran late, I got down to the theatre much after my time. "Where have you *been?*" he demanded indignantly. I explained the subway trouble, but he wouldn't take any excuse, and he bawled the living hell out of me. I just looked at him. "Now, get that broom and sweep the stage!" he said in his best Neronic tones. I picked up the broom at once, jammed it at him and said, "Sweep it yourself, you son of a bitch!," and walked out.

But there was relief the following year, and it came because of my hair. Maxwell Anderson had written a play, *Outside Looking in,* based on the autobiography of writer-hobo Jim Tully. One of the leading characters was "Little Red," and because there were virtually only two actors in New York with red hair, Alan Bunce and myself, there wasn't much competition. I assume I got the part because my hair was redder than Alan's. The show opened at the Greenwich Village Theatre on Seventh Avenue in September 1925. One of the producers was Eugene O'Neill, and he came backstage one night, looked at me, and said nothing. I suspect that was because he had nothing to say. In any case, the play got fine notices (Charles Bickford played the lead), and from the tiny 299-seat house in the Village we moved uptown to the capacious Thirty-ninth Street Theatre, where I had no trouble projecting my voice because of my ample vaudeville experience. After the first act in the new theatre, Maxwell Anderson came backstage and said, "Gather around, boys, gather around." We gathered. "Now I want everybody here to speak twice as loud and twice as fast. You hear?" Then, seeing me, he said, "Everybody, that is, except you."

Outside Looking in ran about four months, and then my Bill and I trekked back to vaudeville. In 1927, we did an act written by Paul Girard Smith called *Lonesome Manor,* a comedy routine about a city hick and a country girl. The scene is Forty-third Street and Broadway, where the out-of-town papers are sold. I come on and the newsboy asks me to hold down the stand for him while he goes to get a cup of coffee. When I'm alone, this little girl from Kokomo, Indiana, (my Bill) comes on, wants to buy the hometown newspaper. And the city hick, true to his city style, has to give her a nickname, so he says, "Well, Koke—tell you what to do." And such-like palaver with a crossfire of jokes and then I sell her the paper, followed by both of us going into a dance—she singing "There's No Place like Home" as her homesick counter melody to my

Oh, there's no doubt about it
And I cannot live without it,
So I simply want to shout it night and day;
There's just one place I want to be
And that's the place that's haunting me—
                              taunting me—
And that's Broadway.

Oh, a million lights, a million sights,
A million ways to spend your nights.
And when I die, I surely want to go
And join that gang below,
For there'll be a bunch I know
From old Broadway.

We wound up with a dance that got us off nicely. My Bill was a
fine dancer, and I worked very hard to learn my job so that we
could make it into the better theatres. We worked the bill with
people like Van and Schenck, Bill Robinson, Ken Murray, and
Buster West. I was simply a hard-working hoofer who worked at
it because he loved it—a dancer at heart.

That was why I felt so good about my next step-up. Or what
I thought would be a step-up. In the 1926–27 New York season,
George Abbott and Phil Dunning's play *Broadway* was the
biggest hit in town. Its leading character was Roy Lane, described by the authors as "a typical song and dance man." When
William A. Brady thought of producing the play, I had been the
first one under consideration for the role. But then Jed Harris
bought the play and hired that very good actor, Lee Tracy, to
play Roy Lane. Lee could act the part beautifully—and did—but
he was no dancer and certainly knew nothing of vaudeville
firsthand. Because both these things were in my bones, I felt that
I had an approach to Roy Lane somewhat like a homing pigeon's
to his coop.

I was, however, cast for Roy in the upcoming London company of the show (my Bill was to be a dancer in it), and as rehearsals began, I was made very uncomfortable by the manage-

ment's insistence that I imitate Lee Tracy. I couldn't imitate Tracy because, fine actor though he was, he was kind of an ungainly fella. The day before sailing for England there was a dress rehearsal of the show with approximately a thousand actors in the audience, one of them a man who was to become an old and much-valued pal, Bob Montgomery. I was terribly uncomfortable through the performance because I had the nagging feeling of an invisible someone tugging at my coattails. Do it this way, do it that way. What was tugging at me was the specter of Lee Tracy's performance. But I got through it well enough, and apparently my very discriminating audience approved. But Jed Harris told me I couldn't play the role in London after all. My Bill withdrew from the London company, and because we both had run-of-the-play contracts, remained in New York—I as Lee Tracy's understudy.

Thirty years later when I was at a dinner party given by my old friends Albert Hackett and Frances Goodrich, Jed Harris came in. He said, "Jim, I'd like to have a sit-down with you to tell you about my situation that time with *Broadway*." I said, "Jed, for God's sake, here we are, old men virtually. Who cares at this point? Actually, Jed, even when it happened, I never gave much of a damn." That surprised Jed, but I was being honest. It was the old in-built Irish don't-give-a-damn speaking.

After *Broadway*, I got into an item called *Women Go on Forever*, starring Mary Boland. Burns Mantle described the show as an opportunity for Miss Boland to forget farce for a while and be joyful over her chance to act a bawdy rooming house keeper who "fights fate, her boarders, and her passions for thirty-six hours." It was around this time that my Bill and I opened a dancing school in Elizabeth, New Jersey. This, one of my great life mistakes, I was inveigled into by a chap who said he would finance it because he considered me a good teacher. (I had previously taught part-time in a New York dancing school.) I would work hard on the teaching in Elizabeth, drink two giant containers of pineapple juice, and then race over to New York to do *Women Go on For-*

ever, something I wasn't able to say about Cagney. It was all exhausting and financially unrewarding as well—although I did have some awfully nice students. One of our seventeen-year-olds went on to become an undertaker, and he moved to Florida, where a year or so ago a man started to go around impersonating me in order to promote real estate. It was my old friend, the undertaker, who sent me clippings to case this pseudo-Cagney down there, and with the clippings he enclosed a short note: "Dear Jim —Just say the word and I'll ship him to you in one of our bye-bye boxes."

My next Broadway show was a successful topical revue, *The Grand Street Follies of 1928*, in which I did some hoofing and a few sketches. This led more or less naturally into *The Grand Street Follies of 1929*, more of the same, and in which I danced briefly to the music of Noël Coward and played a dancing traffic cop. The 1929 revue didn't last long, and I was fortunate on several scores to be cast in George Kelly's play *Maggie the Magnificent*, which opened at the Cort Theatre in October 1929. I say several scores because during this show I met that tremendous gentleman, great playwright, and superb director, George Kelly— and I also met that delightful trouping lady, Joan Blondell. In the show I played a young heel, and Joan was the character comedienne, all gum-chewing and wisecracks and sidelong glances. I also must say I noted at the time that she had a perfectly beautiful body—something my bride knows I've said a number of times. I never knew until some time later why George Kelly cast me in *Maggie the Magnificent*. I was standing outside the theatre with a lot of other actors when he was doing the casting, and he seemed to single me out quite directly and without hesitation. Months later I asked him the reason. He said, "I looked out through the stage door, saw you in that crowd of actors waiting there, and I asked that you be sent in directly. You were *just* what we were looking for—a fresh mutt." He probably hit it right on the head.

I'm glad to say I got to know George Kelly well. Years later when Moss Hart was visiting Hollywood, he told me of his great admiration for this charming and intelligent gentleman. Moss knew that George Kelly was not only one of America's best playwrights but a delight socially, so one evening he invited Joan Blondell, my Bill, and me, together with other friends, to a dinner in honor of "G.K." I was most pleased to be there, although I had been in the boxing ring at the studio all day under very hot lights shooting a fight picture. I was bushed, although I tried valiantly not to show it, and after dinner I didn't realize it but I was ready for a two-day nap. Moss at this point got me to one side and said, "Jim, would you ask G.K. to read the first act of *The Torchbearers* for us?" I felt more than a little diffident about asking Kelly to read his riotously funny comedy, which immortalizes the travails of all amateur theatricals everywhere, and I said so to Moss. But Moss insisted that Kelly wouldn't do it for anyone but me. Finally I agreed.

"Oh, James, James," G.K. said in answer to my request, waving a deprecating hand.

"It would be great for us, G.K.," I said. "I can't tell you how much we'd all love it."

So I talked him into it. Moss got out a copy of the play, and we all sat down expectantly, no one more full of anticipation than Cagney. I sat down three feet away from G.K. Then he began to speak in his soft, gentle voice, and he had uttered perhaps ten words when the rigors of my working day caught up with me. As I was looking G.K. right in the eye in high expectation, my head snapped forward in deep sleep. However I caught myself, straightened up vigorously—and two seconds later my head fell back the *other* way. Out. Completely. To show you the kind of man George Kelly was, this utterly delighted him.

Another thing about George Kelly. Let it be said that I learned from him what a director was for and what a director could do. I have met few really first-rate directors in my life, and those I know, I measure against the very best, George Kelly and John Cromwell. John directed *Women Go on Forever,* and what he and George Kelly shared is something so rare among directors

7. One of the few—perhaps the only Irish actor—able to read this Jewish-directed advertisement for *Taxi!* (1932) was its star.

8. With Ruby Keeler, Joan Blondell, Frank McHugh, and Dick Powell. *Footlight Parade*, 1933.

9. Two years after the grapefruit, Mae Clarke is still getting a hard time. *Lady Killer*, 1933.

10. "Bill" and Jim, 1935.

11. During the filming of *Devil Dogs of the Air* (1935), Amelia Earhart paid a visit to the Warner's lot. Flanking her are would-be flyers O'Brien and Cagney; to the right, unidentified Air Force general in mufti.

12. The bottomless Bottom. *A Midsummer Night's Dream*, 1935.

13. The hoofer—high and hard at work. Rehearsing for *Something to Sing About*, 1937.

14. In *Something to Sing About* came the inspiring opportunity to work with the two dancers he most admired, Johnny Boyle and Harland Dixon, left and right of Cagney.

as to be virtually nonexistent. That something is just this: they were directors who could play all the parts in the play better than the actors cast for them. I'll talk a bit later about a number of Hollywood folk who were called directors, but for the nonce I'll say only that working with a master director like George Kelly was an abiding privilege. On *Maggie the Magnificent's* first day of rehearsal, he said to us, "Now, boys and girls, we have hired you because we know you are experienced. I want the full benefit of all that experience. We think you know your business. Anything that occurs to you, please let me know—because I can't think of everything. So—if you would do me the favor of speaking up? All right now, let's go to work." Naturally, with such a complete professional in control, there was no need for us to give him anything.

What we could have used were audiences. It opened the night of the 1929 market crash. The play closed in a very few weeks. It was about this time that my Bill gently withdrew from our profession. One of the best buck dancers I've ever seen and a genuine talent all down the line, but the show business thing with her was never very strong. She loved it in the beginning, but when she saw some of the sordidness of it, she backed away. A few words of mine about the daily hubbub in Chasen's Restaurant years later puts the business in proper perspective from her point of view:

> Loud, above the talk of pictures and taxes,
> One hears the incessant grinding of axes.

A few months after *Maggie the Magnificent* folded, I was cast in Marie Baumer's *Penny Arcade,* which had all the earmarks of a flop because it lasted only three weeks on Broadway. Yet *Penny Arcade* was for me a sterling success because it became my clear path to the high road. I was reunited with my new old pal, Joan Blondell, once again playing a smart-cracking gal, and I was a sniveling murderer. We were directed by that good man, Bill Keighley. Our reviews were fine and we were looking forward to a good run when the play closed. But Al Jolson had seen the play, liked it, and took an option on it for pictures. This was the beginning of Hollywood for me, and for Joan too, because on Jolson's recommendation we were given an offer from Warner Brothers to re-create our original roles. I came out on a three-week guarantee and I stayed, to my absolute amazement, for thirty-one years.

❧ 3 ❧

Warner Brothers had signed me up for three weeks at five hundred dollars a week, quickly followed by a second three-week contract, again at five hundred dollars. Came then a long-term contract of four hundred dollars a week for forty weeks—or that's what the verbiage seemed to say. Forty-week contract, my foot! The studio had the sole and very handy option of dropping me at the end of any forty-week period, while I was enchained for seven long years.

I wasn't aware of this right at the beginning of my stay there in 1930. Many of us who came West then didn't think we were going to stay. When Clark Gable came to California he was talking to Ralph Bellamy one day in a little coffee shop on Hollywood Boulevard. He said, "Ralph—this thing can't last, you know. It can't last." Ralph asked why, and Clark said simply because of the way they threw money around. "For example," Clark said, "I'm getting eleven thousand dollars for playing a heavy in my current thing. How long do you think that can go on? As a matter of fact, I'm so *sure* that it won't go on that I'm not going to buy anything—*anything*—that I can't take back with me on the train."

I felt this way, and for a considerable period of time. *Sinner's Holiday* was the new title for *Penny Arcade*, with Joan and me in our old roles. We shot the thing in three weeks. The leading man was Grant Withers, a tall, handsome, talented fella, then married to Loretta Young. With my pale New York complexion, which has no pigment except for my freckles, I looked like a wraith, espe-

~ 38 ~

cially opposite Joan, who has a naturally vigorous color. So they had to pile the makeup on me, almost making me Indian red. One day I was standing without makeup behind Grant as he was playing poker between shots. He looked up at me, did a triple-take, and finally realized who I was. "Holy geeze—" he said, "get a load of him without any eyebrows."

The role of my mother in *Sinner's Holiday* was played by an old gal, Lucille LaVerne, a kind of farm-woman type. Lucille had forearms rather like Jim Jeffries', and at one point in the film she was required to hit me. I explained to her that the easiest way to make it look authentic without hurting either of us was for her to hit me with her four fingers, thumb excluded. She agreed, but didn't control it, and the heel of her hand hit me on the jaw, belting me to a fare-thee-well. This was the first of a number of on-camera clouts I was to receive through the years, all to be filed under "hazards of the trade." There was a great vogue then for pictures with "holiday" in the title, and *Sinner's Holiday* was a part of that trend. That title had as much to do with the picture as Winnie-the-Pooh.

A thing that made equal sense was Lew Ayres being cast in the leading role in the next job, *Doorway to Hell*. At the time Lew, in his midtwenties, was one of the prettiest guys in all Hollywood. Notwithstanding, this fine-looking lad was given the role of a latter-day Capone, a ruthless, murdering gangster baron—and I played his quiet pal. That will indicate how they did things at the studios then. Lew was hot at the box office.

While we were shooting, Warner's came to me with a long-term contract. But even then I didn't for a minute think this was going to be my future. As nearly as I could see, the only permanent people at Warner's and other studios were those in the production departments. This was quite a different show business world from the one I had known on Broadway. People in the picture business were of a different stripe entirely from stage people. In the theatre we had our sharpies, but when you got to Hollywood you knew at once you had arrived in the big league for con men and frauds. My very first impression of Hollywood was the same for any other town I had encountered in vaudeville—just a place to do your job. But after a while, I began to realize how sadly obsessed these Hollywood people were with their careers.

I remember one gal who absolutely *cast* her dinner parties. Quite openly she said, "Nobody ever darkens my door who can't improve Sam's business situation." There was also a typically ambitious girl at a dinner party seated opposite a man named Jimmy Kern. She laid on the graciousness by the shovel load for over an hour, and when a pal came over and called him "Jimmy," she was startled. Wasn't he, she asked him, Jerry Kern—*Jerome* Kern? No. With that, she hauled off and belted him right in the puss. He had been wasting her time. Objectivity had no room in her life.

One of my anchors to objectivity in both my work and my life has been poetry. Over the years I've gotten in the habit of putting in verse many of my reactions to the world as I've encountered it, and I must say I've had a lot of fun doing so. Indeed,

> Making verses I cannot help,
> As a pregnant female her brood must whelp,
> Each will come in its given time,
> So there's naught to do but write and rhyme.

My poetic range of interest is pretty broad. One of my Bill's favorites is called *Feet*, which stemmed from the continuing complaint of a friend of ours about her feet, my feet, everybody's feet. This lady hated feet because she thought them ugly in every particular. So I wrote this to her:

> Feet are most unhappy things,
> Encased in leather, tied with strings;
> Made to conform at an early age
> From passing fashion to current rage.
>
> Painted one year, rounded next;
> By corns and bunions ever vexed.
> Toenails dreading the toenail clippers,
> Seeking only the peace of bedroom slippers.

One of the concomitants to my fairly well-developed imagination is the ability to see the oddest things in every shape and shadow. In fact,

> Wherever I look, I see a shape.
> A moving shadow can be an ape,
> A horse, a cow, or a vinegaroon.
> Can it be that sanity's leaving me soon?
> The last one looked like good St. Michael
> Going like hell on a unicycle.
> Maybe sanity's gone, and I don't know it;
> Though generally speaking a person will show it
> In voice or eye or eccentric motion
> To give the viewer a kind of notion
> That something has happened within the brain—
> A possible scar from some bygone strain.
> One just passed! A two-headed figure:
> One head was big, the other bigger.
> A Proteus came and I sought to show him
> The wonderful things my eye perceives,
> But he had changed and gone
> Before I could know him—
> His place quick taken by Eves without leaves.
> And Kim and Marilyn *sans* breek or clout
> Are all right here when I'm far out.

I've been writing verse of sorts since my Broadway days, a habit triggered by reading Stephen Vincent Benét's magnificent *John Brown's Body*. I was also much stimulated by Hugh Kingsmill's *Anthology of Invective and Abuse* and its gems like Blake's onslaught on a gentleman named Kromeck, who was reputed to have made passes at Mrs. Blake:

> A petty sneaking knave I knew—
> Oh,—Mr. Kromeck, how do you do?

Which I should think took care of Mr. Kromeck thenceforth. Robbie Burns was also good at this sort of thing, and I suspect it was Blake and Burns who gave me food for thought when I became fed up with one Hollywood character. This congenital yes-man earned a very high salary by making a profession of soft-soaping. I said of him

> Where once were vertebrae is now a tangle,
> From constant kissing at an awkward angle.

Which describes that lad thoroughly. My brother Ed used to call them the *avec* type. They were always *with* somebody.

I've had a marvelous good time through the years doing these bits, and they principally spring from matters of the moment. Once I was standing talking to Bob Montgomery when a pheasant sounded in the woods, and Bob turned to say—very, very affectionately—"I hear you, I hear you." That made me write

> A pheasant called in a distant thicket,
> And lovingly my old friend said,
> "I hear you, I hear you."
> And he loved that bird, till he gunned him dead.

Very few of my verses are written down, but I've got quite a number stored in my memory. They go the whole gamut of life. There's

> A lady spider met a fella
> And made all haste to date him;
> She loved him with a love sublime,
> Up to and including—
> The time, when in ecstasy,
> She ate him.

And also there was the time years ago when I was driving down Coldwater Canyon in Beverly Hills, came to a red light, and saw Bogart there in a brand new Porsche or some singularly fancy sports car. I have to preface this by saying that Bogie had a nervous habit of picking his nose wherever he was. So there I saw him, stopped for this red light, in this very fancy open car, picking his nose with great industry, little realizing I was watching him. The next day I wrote him this little note:

> In this silly town of ours,
> One sees odd primps and poses;
> But movie stars in fancy cars,
> Shouldn't pick their famous noses.

I never got an answer.

At times, of course, anger can move me to verse. My Bill and I were in Rome with the Ralph Bellamys when the shocking news of Clark Gable's death came. All of that wonderful vitality ceasing so early so suddenly made me think of his stature in the movies and of the powerful men at MGM who controlled his destinies:

> The King, long bled, is newly dead.
> Uneasily wore his crown, 'tis said;
> Quite naturally, since it was made of lead;
> On those who gathered about his throne,
> Y-clept Mayer, Mannix, Katz, and Cohn
> He spat contempt in generous doses,
> But whatever he gave, they made their own.
>
> Unhappy man, he chose seclusion,
> To the unremitting crass intrusion
> Of John and Jane whose names meant dough
> To Louie, Eddie, Sam, and Joe.

The Hollywood whirligig was getting to me, too, in my early movie days when it seemed as if the Warner boys were confusing their actors with their race horses. The pace was incredible. I think I did about six pictures in the first forty weeks. There were professional compensations, of course, like working with a master actor, George Arliss—a most pleasant, very dignified man with an imperturbable manservant named Jenner. Jenner was the very model of the perfect English valet. Mr. Arliss worked diligently from nine in the morning until four in the afternoon, but come four o'clock, Jenner would appear on the hour's stroke, walk right into the set in the middle of a shot if need be, and remove Mr. Arliss' hat or outer garment. Then Jenner would walk off with the item, and this signified the absolute end of shooting for the day. That became an Arliss tradition.

In *The Millionaire,* my only picture with George Arliss, I played a fast-talking insurance man who has to sell a policy and warn Mr. Arliss that he is getting nothing out of life in his retirement. That was my only scene with this great star, and it lasted just two minutes. I wanted it to be good. In the scene, he sits with a shawl about his shoulders, and during the rehearsal, I said, "Mr. Arliss, may I adjust your shawl if it falls down off your shoulders?" He said, "Young man, you do anything you like. I trust your judgment implicitly." Which I thought was awfully nice coming from a grand old trouper to a young guy just beginning to get warm in the business.

Then came *The Public Enemy.* The story was about two street pals—one soft-spoken, the other a really tough little article. For some incredible reason, I was cast as the quiet one; and Eddie Woods, a fine actor but a boy of gentle background, well-spoken and well-educated, became the tough guy. Fortunately, Bill Wellman, the director, had seen *Doorway to Hell,* and he quickly became aware of the obvious casting error. He knew at once that I could project that direct gutter quality, so Eddie and I switched roles after Wellman made an issue of it with Darryl Zanuck.

The picture had its hazards, among them real bullets. This was before the special-effects boys learned how to make "exploding" bullets safe as cap guns. At the time Warner's employed a man named Bailey who had been a machine gunner in World War I, and this boy knew how to make that instrument perform. He sat with the machine gun on a platform above as I skittered along and then ducked down the street behind a "stone" wall. Seconds after I did this, Bailey opened up on the edge of the wall. It crumbled to sawdust, and so would I, had I been there two seconds before.

Another little uncomfortable moment came when that good

actor, Donald Cook, who was my brother in the film, had to display his war-shattered nerves by hauling off and hitting me in the mouth. I think he had some coaching. I've always suspected that Bill Wellman said to him, "Go ahead, let him have it. He can take it," because when Donald belted me, he didn't pull a thing. Instead of faking it as one always does, he just punched me straight in the mouth, broke a tooth, and knocked me galley west.

Public Enemy had a fine cast: Eddie, Donald, Mae Clarke, and the unforgettable Jean Harlow. Borrowed just for that picture, she was a very, very distinct type of gal. Brand new in the business, she didn't much know the acting end, but she certainly was a personality *and* very pleasant to work with. I never saw her after *Public Enemy,* but I was saddened at her death, a needless death as I understand it, because she neglected a serious gall bladder condition.

When Mae Clarke and I played the grapefruit scene, we had no idea that it would create such a stir. This bit of business derived from a real incident in Chicago when a hoodlum named Hymie Weiss was listening to his girl friend endlessly yakking away at breakfast one morning. He didn't like it, so he took an omelet she had just prepared and shoved it in her face. Repeating this on the screen would have been a shade too messy, so we used the grapefruit half. I was not to hear the end of that little episode for years. Invariably whenever I went into a restaurant, there was always some wag having the waiter bring me a tray of grapefruit. It got to be awfully tiresome, although it never stopped me from eating it in the proper amount at the proper time.

A little-known sidelight to the grapefruit scene is that Mae was then married to Monte Brice, Fanny's brother. Mae and Monte had divorced, and apparently with a little rancor, because every time I'd push the grapefruit into Mae's face at the Strand Theatre, there was a guaranteed audience of one—Monte. He would come in just before the scene was shown, gloat over it, then leave.

Public Enemy was one of the first low-budget million-dollar grossers in the business. I'm usually not too much concerned with business details, but in this instance I know just how much the film cost because Bill Wellman told me. The whole thing came in for $151,000, and it took us just twenty-six days to make.

After *Public Enemy* was released, Warner's gave me star billing, which was pleasant enough but hardly compensation for the lack of compensation. I kept grinding the pictures out, working at a swift tempo, and seeing everywhere about me the rough-handed treatment of actors by management. Actors were considered to be expendable material, just like props or makeup. I watched this, and I was to remember.

Meanwhile, the quickies rolled on. In my second Hollywood year, 1931, came *Smart Money*, the only picture I ever made with that fine gentleman and splendid actor, Edward G. Robinson. Again Eddie was a gangster, again I was a pal—his pal. It seems to me I was playing an awful lot of pals those days. I saw *Smart Money* not long ago because I was curious about it. A solid number of my pictures I've never seen, and some of the ones I have seen satisfied my curiosity about them in a single showing or even halfway through. Anyway, looking at *Smart Money* gave me the pleasure of seeing Eddie as his usual sharp self, that always solidly reliable self.

Next came *Blonde Crazy*, in which I played a red-hot bellhop loaded for larceny, sharing it all as ever with Joan Blondell. This was the first time I had ever worked with Louis Calhern, a very suave gent and excellent light comedian, who made a very interesting observation to me at the time. He said, "You sawed-off fellas have to make it. When I went into the business, they needed tall leading men for those strong, forceful leading women—Ethel Barrymore, Margaret Anglin, and the like—all tall gals. I was six foot four, and that's what producers wanted. Guys a few inches under six feet wouldn't get the roles; you fellas have to make it."

But 1931 wasn't all push and rush. There were some very tangible personal rewards, the nicest of them the arrival of my brother, Bill, in California. He hadn't been feeling too well back East so he came out to get some rest as well as visit us. RKO saw him, said he looked like Jim Cagney, which he sure as hell did, and they tested him. It was a success, and he did a few pictures, but his heart wasn't in them. So with that astute business mind at hand, and my needing very badly an astute business mind, he became my business manager, and we haven't looked back since.

Also that year, I joined The Players. That venerable club on New York's Gramercy Park has been a continuing source of friendship and laughter for me down through the years. Always when I go there, I find a lively *stammtisch* of good talk and high-flying wit, most frequently featuring the delightful insult. Not long ago, I was sitting there with my old pal Roland Winters, chatting away, when a friend of ours—St. John Tyrell, pronounced "Sinjin"—dropped by to join in the conversation. Only "inundate" might be more fitting than "join in." Also at our table were Davie Doyle and a few others. Rolie and Davie were trying to get in a word or two, but our fast-talking friend was having none of it. He was, he is, a perfectly wonderful guy but, as the old phrase has it, he does go on. Finally, Rolie looked at him and said, "I'll *pee* on you!" To which Davie Doyle replied, "No—his book is filled." The Players always freshens me each time I get back to New York.

As my first months in Hollywood rolled on, the work schedule continued very much as before, and clearly the nicest thing about it all was working with some very talented and very personable people. There were exceptions. I am thinking of one actress who had reached the top, not a very strong talent, and who possessed a presence that constantly reassured you of her eminence. I didn't like her because once on a set she had been nasty to a friend of mine—a warm, gentle person. After she blasted him, I wrote a few lines about her.

THE ARTISTE

One views the form and finds it fair,
The face decided comely,
Though without a jot of stick and pot
They say she's rather homely.

~ 47 ~

Performancewise there's ne'er a change,
No matter what the part is.
When one perceives so spare a range,
One wonders where the art is.

By dint of constant labor,
She parlayed little into much:
There were stocks and bonds, annuities,
Real estate and such.

She handled each transaction
With shrewdness and with tact,
But she'd give it all up happily,
If only she could act.

Still, her number was in the distinct minority among my working companions.

One of my nicest working companions I met in 1931 when I was doing *Taxi!*. This was George Raft, who shared with me the New York street background and professional dancing experience. In *Taxi!* there was going to be a dance contest featuring that intricate step I knew so well, the Peabody. Georgie was newly arrived in town, had done little in pictures, and I felt sure he was the only other one in California who knew the Peabody well. So I told the assistant director to find George for my rival in the dance contest. This he did, and that was a most effective little scene.

It was also in *Taxi!* that I had an adventure bordering on misadventure. From my taxi I had to fire two shots out of the window and duck; then a machine gun would cut loose and take the window out over my head. The scene was played as called for with one exception: one of the machine-gun bullets hit the head of one of the spikes holding the backing planks together. It ricocheted and went tearing through the set, smacked through a sound booth, ripped across the stage, hit a clothes tree, and dropped into the pocket of someone's coat. I was young enough not to consider this pretty dangerous activity.

My next picture, *The Crowd Roars,* was a pretty vigorous Howard Hawks production in which I played a race driver. My buddy on the tracks was Frank McHugh, who soon enough became my buddy in real life. This was the first time I worked with Frank, although I had met him previously a few times back East. Now I got to know him well, and that friendship has been one of life's real joys.

After our first day of shooting on *The Crowd Roars,* Frank and I shared a suite at the Santa Barbara Hotel. We were just getting acquainted, so to speak, and we *spoke.* We stayed up the entire night and talked. We talked until we had to go to work the next morning. Which will give some idea of the many things we had in common. We worked the next day through without sleep, but we were young and thought little of it.

One delightful incident in Frank's early life in pictures then occurred when he ran into an old character actor called Forrester Harvey. Frank mistook him for another Hollywood old-timer, Joseph M. Kerrigan. At the same time Harvey more understandably took Frank for his brother, Matt McHugh. As Frank and Harvey reminisced about past shared experiences, they both became aware that somehow their conversation wasn't making much sense. Nevertheless they went manfully ahead, recalling shows they thought they had done together. After they said goodbye, Harvey said to himself, "Matt is drinking too much." Frank said to himself sadly, "Poor old Joe is getting old."

One time, when I was doing a picture with Frank, an interviewer was researching a piece on me, and I said, "For God's sake, there's a story on this set that nobody touches. It's a great story—the story of the McHugh family." But as far as I know no one has ever written in any detail about that wonderful bunch of people. They were *all* in the theatre. Frank's mother and father were traveling actors—with five progeny all in the same troupe with them. Jim, their eldest, was a leading man, and the others— Matt, Kitty, Ed, and Frank—played supporting roles. They did musicals, dramas, melodramas, farces—they did it all, and nothing was left out of their theatrical background.

So when the McHughs came into the picture business, they had unparalleled experience to draw on. Frank was the youngest of the family, and he played everything, every conceivable sort of role. Put Frank into a scene with a newcomer, and he would make that newcomer look much better than he had any right to look. This was what made Frank so important at Warner Brothers.

There is in his acting a very warm and methodical determination that is really a reflection of the man he is in real life. He lives happily now in retirement at Cos Cob, Connecticut. Not long ago he went into his bank there, and in the window saw a sign announcing the gift of a free cookbook with each new hundred-dollar account. What an opening for Frank! He walked in promptly, made out a check for a hundred dollars, and opened a new account, or so he thought. The girl behind the wicket, knowing him as a valued customer, said, "Thank you, Mr. McHugh. I'll file that." Very seriously Frank asked for his cookbook, and the girl was startled, explaining that cookbooks were only given for new accounts, not to old customers. Frank explained patiently that he had just given her a hundred dollars for a *new* account. "But you don't understand—" the girl said. "I understand very well," said Frank. "I understand that the *old* money is no good. That's what you're telling me. And you're telling me that only the *new* money gets a cookbook."

She tried to explain it very carefully to him, and he just as carefully explained to her that he was following the letter of the bank's law about new accounts, thus warranting him the cookbook. Wearily the girl called over the manager who said, "Well, Mr. McHugh, you see—" "Please don't give me the 'you see,'" said Frank. "Give me the cookbook. I'm now beginning to wonder whether what you're doing is just trying to stay in business, because whenever we had trouble in the picture business, we gave away dishes. *Are* you having trouble? I can go down the street, make a hundred-dollar deposit in another bank, and get a cookbook down *there*." Frank was having a ball, asking for the cookbook as they tried to outtalk him. He didn't get the cookbook, but he had a lot of fun—and who knows? Maybe he was right. The payoff to this story came some time later when his bank had another ad in the window. This time it was for a fountain pen, to be given for availing oneself of a particular bank service. The same girl Frank had talked to before saw him reading the new ad, so when he stepped up to her window, she said quickly, "Here, Mr. McHugh," and handed him the fountain pen.

In and around the time I was making *The Crowd Roars* with Frank, my troubles with the studio front office became more persistent. These troubles surfaced when I realized that there were roughly two classes of stars at Warner's: those getting $125,000 a picture—and yours sincerely, who was getting all of $400 a week. And that $400 soon stopped because I walked. After that little squabble was patched up, Warner's some while later gave me another solid reason to walk out. They ignored my contract by billing another name over mine at the Warner Theatre in Hollywood. This reaction was no flowering of Cagney vanity: top billing is an entitlement that means money in the bank, and I was protecting my entitlement. A photograph was taken of the offending marquee, and in the ensuing lawsuit, the judge found for me.

I did an entire series of these walkouts over the years. I walked out because I depended on the studio heads to keep their word on this, that, or other promise, and when the promise was not kept, my only recourse was to deprive them of my services. I'd go back East and stay on my farm until we had some kind of understanding. I'm glad to say I never walked out in the middle of a picture, the usual procedure when an actor wanted a raise. Moreover, I got solid support from people in my profession. Freddie March, for instance, came to testify for me in one of my suits against Warner Brothers, and I have been told that outside the courthouse, Freddie was warned by a prominent director that such testimony would be very bad for his career. It took guts and real staunchness for Freddie to appear and say all he had to say.

It wasn't until some of us began to do a little walking out that the studios' total dictatorship over talent began to diminish. The standard employment formula was this: long-term contracts, many of them for seven years, with the studio having the option to drop or employ periodically during that time—and if a player walked, the time he was out would be added on to the term of the contract. This is what happened to Olivia de Havilland and Bette Davis; and the studio, having tremendous clout in the courts, usually won, forcing the actors back to do films they despised. What is usually not realized is that most of the scripts we were forced to do were acutely dreadful. Once I got such a script and asked the producer if he had read it. "Of course I've read it," he said. Genuinely incredulous, I said, "Do you really want to do it?" He said, "We've got to do it. The picture is already sold. We've got a million-dollar profit in the kitty already—before the first camera rolls. What are you going to do—argue with a million bucks?"

The picture turned out to be a miserable thing and I didn't enjoy it, but at that early point in my career I was doing it for a living, which means you do as required, and what the hell? Around this time a Boston exhibitor told me that I was carrying quite a load. Naïvely I asked him what he meant, and he broke the facts of life about block booking to me. The exhibitor explained that he bought some pictures from my studio, and in his words, "I had to take five dogs to get one Cagney film." This was block booking—the shenanigan by which an exhibitor was forced to take a lot of what he didn't want in order to get what he did want. Gradually when I began to understand more and more of these cute studio devices, my education began!

But in the early 1930s I was still learning, and I went along making what was given me. In 1932, I did a fight picture, *Winner Take All*, which gave me the chance to meet one of the few Hollywood characters ever to merit that misused and overused word, "fabulous." This was Wilson Mizner, the great raconteur and adventurer in living, who helped write the picture. Bill Mizner was fascinating to hear, fascinating to see. He had a high, reedy voice, wore loose dentures, and obviously had seen and done much in his life. During the picture I did my fights and trained with an ex-welterweight, Harvey Perry. Once when we were taking off our bandages, Bill piped, "How're your hands, Jamesie?" I said, "My hands are all right, Bill. I broke one hand when I was about fifteen or so, but they're fine now." Next Bill asked Harvey how his were, and they were fine, too. Then Bill said, "Look at mine." I have never seen such hands in my life. They looked as if someone had battered them with a sledgehammer—all the metacarpals busted—*both* hands. I said, "In the name of God, Bill, how did you get those?" "Oh," he said, "hitting whores up in Alaska."

Some people are called characters and don't merit the designation. Wilson Mizner was a genuine character. We would go in to have a story conference for the picture but there'd be no conference. We'd sit and listen—and all of it was delightful.

While we were shooting *Winner Take All,* a professional fighter who had been watching me in the ring at the studio came up to me and said, "So you know how to use your dukes, that's possible for an amateur to do. But where'd you get your footwork? Don't gimme that amateur crap now. You say you *wasn't* a professional—with that footwork?" When I told him I had never been a pro, that I had been only a street fighter and the closest I ever got to the ring was as a kid watching my idol, Packy Mac-Farland, this fighter refused to believe it. So I explained. I said, "Tommy, I'm a *dancer.* Moving around is no problem." "Oh," he said. "I get it. When I first saw you doing your stuff, I said this son-of-a-bitch has been at it. Now I get it."

Not long after *Winner Take All* was *Picture Snatcher,* with its fairly interesting title, which designated my job in the film. I played a former crook who "straightens out" and takes up work as a picture-snatcher. This was a man hired by a newspaper to steal photographs of people who are trying to keep those photographs out of the paper. By this time—1933—we were shooting movies in seventeen days, eighteen days, twenty-one days. Hell, we could have *phoned* them in. Lloyd Bacon actually shot *Picture Snatcher* in fifteen days. I used to kid him by saying, "What are you doing —getting a bonus for bringing it in ahead of schedule?"

One of those fifteen days I was just walking through a scene with Ralph Bellamy, laying out what I was going to do. I stood outside a door waiting for my cue, bounced in, and went to

Ralph's desk. We did our words, there was also a phone call during it, and then I had some more words, and then out of the room. Suddenly I heard Lloyd yell, "Cut—print it!" I said, "Hey, you—I was rehearsing!" "It looked fine from here," he said. *That* was the ultimate efficiency—shooting a damned rehearsal!

There was another unhappy moment for me in *Picture Snatcher*. That cute little gal, Alice White, played one of the girls, and inasmuch as I now had a reputation in pictures as a woman slugger, the following was set up: Alice was supposed to come at me as I sat in an open car and say, "Hello, Danny," while I was waiting for Patricia Ellis, who was my girl. Alice then climbs into the car, says, "Aren't you going to kiss me?" and I reply, "Get lost, will ya?" Then she reaches over, starts to kiss me, I push her away, she slaps me hard on the face. The projected business then was for me to hit her in retaliation, but of course I never hit anybody with a real punch. I never closed my hand into a fist. It might have looked closed to the audience, but it wasn't. So, getting ready for this shot, I said to her, "Now, Alice, don't you do a thing." Lloyd Bacon reaffirmed that: "Alice, don't you do a thing. Jim will not hit you. We want to get a good shot, and Jim will make it look good. From the camera angle we've got now, everything is going to be fine. So don't pull *too* far away—Jim will let his fist go right by you."

Well, nice little Alice wanted to make sure that she wasn't doing the wrong thing, so she got everything in the sequence of action correct except the last bit. Instead of pulling away slightly, she stuck her chin *out* and I really goaled her. "Cut!" And there was poor little Alice down on the floor of the car, crying her heart out. I asked her why she had stuck her chin out. She didn't answer that but sobbed, "And I thought *Talbert* could hit!" Now, Mr. Talbert was her sweetheart or perhaps her husband at the time, and it didn't seem tactful to continue that particular line of conversation. I was mighty sorry to have hit that cute little kisser.

Our director, Lloyd Bacon, was a great guy to work with. On receiving a script he wasn't one of those directors who'd say, "When? Where? What? How?" Lloyd would just say "Who?"

"Who?" translates to "Who have I got?," and usually who he got was who he wanted to get—his gang, the stock company: Pat O'Brien, McHugh, Cagney, Allen Jenkins, and others of us who worked so well with each other and with him. It didn't matter what the hell the story was; when we went to bat, we did the best we could.

It was great going to bat for Lloyd, and that's a phrase he'd appreciate, because his most vivid directorial instruction was also taken from baseball. He used to tell us, "Run out your hit!" In professional ball, if a player got a scratch hit that might be fielded easily by the other team, and he failed to run like hell anyway, failed to run it *out*—he could be fined or fired. The sense behind that rule was that you never know what is going to happen to a baseball once it leaves the bat. The opposing player might muff an easy catch, letting it go through his legs; the ball might bounce over his head—any number of possibilities. So if you don't run out your hit, you haven't done your job to the limit.

Lloyd might have learned his persistence and thoroughness from his father, that tremendous actor, Frank Bacon, who after years of work in the small time finally made a great Broadway success with *Lightnin'* in 1918, a performance I saw and admired. Lloyd used "Run out your hit!" advantageously any number of times. A scene might be developing very well, and suddenly because it didn't please one particular player, he would turn his back on it and say, "It's all wrong." Lloyd would shout, "My God, run out your hit! Once you get going, run it out." O'Brien and I, old ballplayers, knew immediately what he meant.

Picture Snatcher was my first picture with that fine boyo, Ralph Bellamy, and in one scene it was required that he hit *me*. Ralph has arms from here to Ashtabula, and he was worried as hell about what he'd do to me. I indicated my chin, told him to aim for it and not to worry. "You won't hit me, so help me," I told him. "You won't hit me." "But I've never thrown a punch in my life," he said, still very worried. Lloyd Bacon called for the camera to roll, and Ralph threw the punch. Well, he certainly aimed at my chin, but he had no control over that far-reaching arm of his. It was simply too long for him to control, and he hit me on the side of the cheek with a closed fist. I went flying across the room, slammed into a chair, pulverized it completely, and in the process broke off another tooth. You have yet to see a more disconsolate man than Ralph Bellamy that day. "I *told* you I've never thrown any punches," he said, "I've never hit anybody in my life." "You sure as hell have now," I told him, "so don't worry about it." "I'll never do it again," he said—and as far as I know he never has.

Making pictures then was a fatiguing business, and in my next, *Mayor of Hell*, it was the old mixture as before, only more so. As a crook who helped reform a reform school, I was kept plenty busy, and I mean literally to all hours. Frequently we worked until three or four in the morning. I'd look over and there'd be the director, Archie Mayo, sitting with his head thrown back, sawing away. He was tired; we were *all* tired. This kind of pressure the studio put on us because they wanted to get the thing done as cheaply as possible. At times we started at nine in the morning and worked straight through to the next morning. This pounding drive we kept up during my time at Warner's from 1930 to 1934 on a pretty unvarying schedule.

The same thing held for *Footlight Parade,* where I at least had the pleasure of dancing. That film brings to mind a question frequently asked of me: Did my height ever give me trouble with leading ladies? Only with one—Claire Dodd, in *Footlight Parade*. She was the tallest of all the ladies I've ever worked with—a tall, handsome gal—and in close shots opposite her, they had to slip a two-inch apple box under me. Which brings me to the subject of my height. For reasons unknown to me, people are always interested in my exact height. The literal truth is, I don't know what it is. I haven't measured for years, and I'm really not interested enough to do so. I do know my wife is five foot one, and I tower over her by a good seven inches.

Various newspaper accounts of my career have pegged my height at different levels, and I think the reason they never agree is because in any fight scene I have always insisted on having an opponent bigger than myself. This came about by a discovery early on that any time I hit anybody my own size it looked as if I was taking advantage of them. I probably was one of the few fellas in the business who had done any degree of boxing and street fighting and who *looked* as if he had done it. My physical deportment made this clear. I have seen lots of leading men then and now who throw punches like a handful of confetti. Really ridiculous. I have always thought if they sign a guy to do a rugged part, they should get him into the gym and just get him used to throwing punches.

Footlight Parade was one of those fluffy musical incredibilities, pure fantasy all the way, but it gave the song-and-dance people a chance to be employed. Little Ruby Keeler danced her heart out, and she knew what she was doing. And as for Dick Powell—people never realized what a good voice that boy had, and a lot of nice things to go with it. I was terribly fond of this nice, nice guy all the years I knew him. When that throat cancer took him, we were devastated because he was a rare one. One of the remarkable people, and Warner's was full of them.

One of many I met there was Lowell Sherman. I had seen Lowell years before in a 1919 Broadway show, *The Sign on the Door*, by Channing Pollock. Lowell was starred with Mary Ryan, and he played the heavy. He was a big, bad, bold seducer who ultimately got his comeuppance in the form of a bullet through the heart at the curtain. But he was so amusing and charming all the time he was being this "dirty despicable dog" that the audience applauded fervidly even after he was shot, so fervidly indeed that he came out and took a bow! That seems a little ridiculous now, but that's what happened those days in the theatre when an actor had a winning way.

So when I saw Lowell in *The Sign on the Door*, I said to myself, "Unh-*huh! That's* how it's done, *that's* the way to do it." In 1919 I knew nothing about, cared nothing about show business, but this actor I remembered. So years later, when I got to Warner Brothers, Lowell was working there. He didn't know me even faintly, and all I knew of him was that here was one hell of an actor. A mutual friend of ours, an agent, got talking to him about playing heavies. Lowell told my friend, "There's a little guy at Warner's now with kind of a funny name. I like the way he does it. He gets his quota of laughs, and at the same time gets in all the nasties." The agent asked him if he meant me, and Lowell said yes. When the agent told me this, I asked him to tell Lowell that I got my first acting lesson watching him play *The Sign on the Door* with Mary Ryan and Lee Baker. I added, "And tell him I thank him now for that lesson."

This was communicated, and Lowell asked to meet me. The agent gave a party for me to meet Lowell, and as I was standing in the middle of the room with a group of people, the doorbell rang. The door burst open and there, flamboyantly, was "Himself." Lowell was a handsome man and there he was, wearing a very expensive Eddie Schmidt suit, handmade shirt, flowing tie, silk handkerchief up the sleeve, *plus* a monocle. I looked at him, he looked at me, and as he strode toward me, he bellowed, "Baaaaaabeeeeee!"

We became good friends, this remarkable man and I. I actually saw him do an almost impossible thing—make a straight man of that incomparable actor, John Barrymore, in a 1929 picture, *General Crack*. Lowell did this by subtly making his straight role, that of a king, into a comedy character. Lowell died in 1934 of throat cancer, the clear result of his chain smoking. A great loss, and he was only in his forties.

I think I partake of his general approach to acting. Margaret Hamilton, that wonderful character actress who played the wicked witch in *The Wizard of Oz*, said when asked about me, "Oh, well—although he became known for other things, he's essentially a comedian. I've always called him a comedian." This I admit to. I've always tried to drop a comic touch here and there in virtually everything I do, I hope with success.

I have, incidentally, a little poem on success. I read a newspaper article about a number of gals interviewed on the subject of masculine sexiness in various walks of life. These ladies agreed generally that good-looking men were sexy, well-dressed men were sexy, but by far the sexiest men were the successful men with lots of money. So I wrote:

> From the lowest pimp to the U.S. prexy,
> The broads do find success is sexy.

You can't fight it, boys.

4

I said the subtitle of this book could well be *The Remarkable People*. Well, one of my remarkable people supplied an alternate subtitle—*The Far-Away Fella*—meaning me. He is about the least far-away fella I know. Pat O'Brien. One would think that someone like me who feels he has something to offer in show business would enjoy the limelight. But of a social evening, especially years ago, I'd never care to get up and entertain because I had no confidence in myself to do that sort of thing. One night when the Masquers Club was giving a pipe night for Frank McHugh, Pat O'Brien called and asked me if I was going to be there. I said I would, but Pat said, "Aw, come on now—you didn't say that very convincingly." I assured him I'd be there, and I asked him why he doubted me. "Because," said Pat, "because you're one of those far-away fellas." One of the things he meant by those words is that I don't follow the cocktail party circuit or do the talk show thing. Certainly in that sense, and perhaps some others, I am a far-away fella, and most people who've been around me for any length of time have come to the same conclusion.*

---

* "I must really insist on footnote space here. What I meant additionally by 'far-away fella' is that this lad Cagney also has a deep strain of altruism running under his words and deeds. Unlike most, he is a thinking man, and a good and kindly one to boot.

—PAT O'BRIEN"

Pat definitely isn't a far-away fella, and he's remarkable in more than one way. He has, for instance, more durability than anyone I've ever known. He would arrive on the set in the morning, having been up all night—clear-eyed, knowing all his words—and step cheerfully in front of the camera. At day's end, home, have dinner; then he and Eloise would go out and would again stay up all night. I am strictly an eight-hours-a-night boy myself.

And by 1934 at Warner's, I sure wasn't getting it. During this time there was *Jimmy the Gent*, my first with a good director I was going to see a lot of, Michael Curtiz. I murdered Mike the first day of that picture with a little incident. When I heard I was going to play another one of *those* guys, I said to myself, "They want another of those mugs, I'll really give them a mug." So I had my head shaved right down to the skull except for a little top knot in front, and I had the makeup man put bottle scars all over the back of my head. The opening shot was of my back to the camera, with all those scars in sharp focus. The phone rings, I turn around to speak—and Mike Curtiz damn near fainted when he saw that shaved head. Hal Wallis, who was running that part of the studio at the time, took my haircut as a personal affront. "What is that son-of-a-bitch trying to do to me now?" he said. To *him*, for God's sake.

My leading lady in *Jimmy the Gent* was Bette Davis, the first time we appeared together. She was unhappy doing the picture because she was waiting impatiently to go to another studio to do *Of Human Bondage*, which was to turn out so well for her. Her unhappiness seeped through to the rest of us, and she was a little hard to get along with. But she was still a pro and did her job beautifully, as she always did and always has done. Years later when I saw her in *All About Eve*, I wrote her a fan letter to end all fan letters. One of the last times I saw her was at an Academy Awards do, where I was presenting one of the awards. The whole business was a cataclysmic foul-up.

Bette was furious. "What is the matter with these people, Jimmy? Why don't they put this thing on like professionals?" I looked at her and said, "Ah, Bette, you still care, huh? You still care?" "You've *got* to care," she said, "everything has to be done right. If it's worth doing at all, it's worth doing well." "Ah, it isn't worth worrying about, sweet," I told her. "Just forget it." But of course she was right. Years later when she wrote her autobiography, I was happy to write a little blurb for it. I said, "One thing you have to understand in all this so-called creative business—all the way from the producer down: the person doing it has to care and care deeply. The artist (that's a much-abused word) cares—he cares, he cares. And the producer-artist, the writer-artist, the director-artist, the actor-artist, the cameraman-artist, each one must care. Caring is the thing. And Davis had that to the utmost. She cared about it every second. And for that I had to admire her."

To return to Pat O'Brien—this was always a fella with the cheeriest kind of upbeat optimism. When we were on location making *Here Comes the Navy,* he and I went down to Rancho Santa Fe to see Bing Crosby's home there. (On location we had one day a week off; back in Hollywood it was frequently seven days a week working in the old Warner's tradition.) Bing wasn't home, but we made ourselves known to the caretakers, who graciously let us wander about that beautiful adobe house. Walls three feet thick keeping it cool inside—exquisite rose gardens, superb bougainvillea trees everywhere, tennis courts and swimming pool—the entire treatment.

Pat said, "Pretty nice, huh, Jim—pretty nice?" But it was better than pretty nice. Pat and I each owned a house, practical but nothing fancy, so I said to Pat, "Well, yes. It's lovely, it's fine, but it's going to be a whole lot harder to give up than ours." He looked at me and said, "Why, you killjoy bastard!"

"Face some facts," I said. "This is one of those businesses when you go to the job, the job stays for a while, and then you're on your way." Pat could never accept my cautious attitude about Hollywood—that house built of cards, as I considered it. Ever the optimist, he felt it was going to go on forever, and for him it did. Pat is still keeping himself busy at seventy-five.

In those early days, I was always the cautious one. In our more serious moments, I'd say, "Pat, stop and take stock. Where do we stand? Is this going to give us security for the rest of our lives?" But Pat never listened. He was for the jokes, the laughter, the nightclubs. The wonderful payoff is that it didn't disagree with him in the slightest. He's my age and looks wonderfully well —still enthusiastically going around the country playing summer theatres, doing his one-man show at colleges and nightclubs, telling the stories, and doing very well indeed. By high contrast, I couldn't care less for this kind of activity. In that sense too I am the far-away fella, far away from the madding crowd as I can get, loving the countryside, the sea, the horses, the cattle, and everything that goes with it.

Two interesting things happened when Pat and I were making *Here Comes the Navy.* One was funny, the other not funny at all. Warner Brothers had some clout with the Navy, and we were allowed to film the battleship *Arizona* with the entire Pacific fleet fanning out behind it. This was a tremendous shot, of course, and when we first saw it on the screen in the rushes we were all just knocked over. Then out of the darkness we heard the screenwriter's voice: "Some piece of writing, huh?" He was serious.

The other incident involved Pat and me. He was a chief petty officer in the picture and I was a gob, assigned to the lighter-than-air group. In one scene Pat is supposed to be handling a rope dangling from the great dirigible *Macon,* when he is hauled off the ground unexpectedly, and must hang on for his life. The script also had me up in the *Macon,* and I was to go down the dangling rope to him and throw another line around his waist, binding him to me. This was being shot from the ground up against the sky, giving the illusion that Pat, the rope, and I were well up in the air. As he was dangling there and I came down the rope, I put my legs around him and suddenly he completely lost his grip. I couldn't support his weight and mine, too, so we both went straight down. Somebody said they could see the smoke coming from my hands as I slid. They put medication on both our hands. Pat's were burned, too, but mine looked like hamburger because I was hanging on tighter. Once more the hazards of the trade.

Speaking of hazards, my next picture, *St. Louis Kid,* in which I was a fighting milk truck driver (whatever the role, I was always fighting), had me at one point encounter a very formidable actor, Robert Barrat. Bob was a physical culturist in real life, and he had a solid forearm the size of the average man's thigh. As I always say to anybody throwing punches at me in a scene, "Just go ahead and throw. I won't be there, I'll be inside it." After saying this to Bob, he threw an overhand right, and I stepped inside it. But I reckoned without that big forearm, which hit me on the side of my head, damn near taking it off. It would have been a hell of a lot easier if he had belted me with his fist.

By the time I was ready to do *St. Louis Kid,* I was so fed up with walking in and punching people again and again that I called in the makeup man and had him wrap my hands in bandages. In the picture's opening scene I come out of a courtroom with my hands in this mummy wrap and let it be known to my perennial sidekick, Allen Jenkins (who was always getting me in trouble in the film), that I was through hitting for him. I had just walked down the courtroom steps, Jenkins had bumped someone's car, and as that driver started to hit Jenkins, I was to step in. Instead of punching, however, I just whipped my head around and hit the guy between his eyes with my forehead. Down he went. For the rest of the picture I went around hitting people with my head, all of this in a specific attempt to vary the old punching formula. I can still hear the reedy voice of *St. Louis Kid's* producer, "When are you going to take those bandages off and start punching right?" This gentleman rather failed to understand what I was trying to do. In his book, I was simply trying to foul up his living.

It was around this time that I joined Screen Actors Guild, joined it in fact during its first months of existence. What most moviegoers of the time did not realize was that actors as a group got less than two cents out of every dollar taken in at the box office. Many actors were lucky to earn sixty-six dollars for a six-day week, and they were forced to work almost every Saturday night and often into the early hours of Sunday. Getting off for a national holiday during the week meant they would have to work the following Sunday without pay to make up for that holiday. The actor was not only low man on the totem pole, he was practically buried in the ground.

So when the Screen Actors Guild came into being in 1933, one thing the producers did not want was for any featured players or stars to come into the group. Therefore they resorted to the hoary old technique of divide and conquer. Their emissaries would say to a Gable, "Aren't you a good friend of Bob Montgomery's?" and Clark would admit it, asking why the question. "Oh, nothing, nothing," would be the answer, and the matter was "dropped." This, of course, stimulating Gable to think, "Now, what the hell did Montgomery say about me?" The studio people would then go to a Tracy and ask him if he was on good terms with Gable, thus working the same game—the whole point of it being to engender mutual suspicion among all the players. When they pulled that on Bob Montgomery, he was a little smarter than the producers thought. Realizing this whole thing was too pat, Bob went to Tracy and Gable and asked them if the producers had been feeding them the same question.

When this was verified, Bob said, "You know, these unprincipled sons-of-bitches are going to do everything they can to keep us at odds with each other." Those divisive tactics were overcome, and the Screen Actors Guild became a potent force in the motion picture industry. The need for the Guild was dramatized for me by that very gentle gentleman, Boris Karloff (Boris playing monsters, by the way, was type casting in reverse). Boris came to me one day saying, "Jim, I'm having a terrible time. Every morning I have to report three and a half hours before work commences in order to put on these fanciful makeups. By day's end, I'm thoroughly exhausted, and then it's another hour getting the damned stuff off. Sometimes they keep me working through to eleven or twelve o'clock at night. It's terribly, terribly trying."

I said, "Boris, this is exactly what they're doing at Warner Brothers, too."

They were squeezing as much out of us as they could— eleven-, twelve-hour days—frequently working nights right through to sunup. This didn't bother the studio heads because they were home with their families having dinner at the appropriate hour. When the Screen Actors Guild demanded an eight-hour day, the producers screamed. Then I discovered a startling statistic: the average actor with screen credit—which means he was something of a name player—worked in the course of one year only an average of *three and a third weeks.* Incredible. So it was pretty thin for a lot of good people all the way, and I personally felt this to be part of the producers' overall plan: keep actors poor so they can't argue about anything. But we did, and we won.

In 1935 I moved into a category some performers prize very highly—the first ten players in box-office popularity. But that kind of thing I found essentially meaningless. I was asked once if I suddenly woke up one day to realize I was famous, a star. Nothing of the sort! I never gave it a thought, never thought of it at all. Whatever was going on in my Hollywood life I regarded as completely transitory. I looked on it only as doing a job, and that job happened to work out. And the answer to all that is, where did I go nights? I sure wasn't going around picking up the kudos— or the kiddos. I just stayed home. I once saw a very well-known playwright at "21" (I was there twice in my life) who came in while I was having dinner with Warner's head publicity man. This writer just had a Broadway hit, and as he walked from table to table, shaking hands and receiving congratulations, I thought how sad it was. He needed that support, all the praise and adulation. He needed it badly, sought it avidly. He savored every bit of that temporary eminence instead of just buckling down and furthering his job. That, I think, is what I did. Just going along year by year, doing my job, nothing more than that.

By 1935, the job was becoming fairly predictable. It was then I did *G-Men,* which was a step up the ladder artistically. There was a great deal of interest at the time in these forceful and thoroughgoing champions of the law, and there was an effort to make the film as authentic as possible. Once again, as in *Taxi!* and *The Public Enemy*, a machine-gun spray was needed, and also once again they used real bullets. At one point in the story, I was behind a wall of fireplace logs. I had some little misgivings about this because the logs were loose, and with the fusillade of bullets due to hit them, anything might happen. So I experienced—and expressed—for the first time at Warner's my misgivings about being shot at. Bill Keighley, the director, said, "I promise you, Jim, the guy firing that gun will not do anything that will injure you." His promise held.

By this time I was referring to these pictures as "cuff operas" because a number of the things in them were ad-libbed, dialogue contributed by the actors and directors right off the cuff. I recall *The Irish in Us* and a scene where Frank McHugh comes in, having been to a formal affair at the Firemen's Ball. He returns home at midnight wearing a full-dress suit and a white cap. Pat O'Brien looks at him and says, "You didn't wear that cap to the ball?" to which Frank improvised the great reply, "Oh, I know, it should have been black?"

There wasn't much ad-libbing allowable in *A Midsummer Night's Dream*, my only excursion into Shakespeare. A year before we did it, there had been a successful Hollywood Bowl presentation of the play directed by Max Reinhardt, and Warner's Hal Wallis decided to re-create it. I think he wanted to do something that had some value to it, something other than the knock-'em-drag-'em-outs we'd been doing for so long. Since he had the Warner's stock company at hand to draw from, people like Joe E. Brown, Dick Powell, Frank McHugh, Olivia de Havilland, Victor Jory—he did it. This was a Max Reinhardt production, but because Reinhardt was essentially a spectacle director not able to appreciate professionally the necessity for minimum movement that film demands, he remained largely on the sideline while Bill Dieterle directed. Reinhardt, so used to broad stage gestures, made some of the actors do things that were, I thought, ridiculous for the screen. We used to stand back, watching him, and say, "Somebody ought to tell him." In any case, Reinhardt was a very nice man, and what with my bum German and his bum English, we managed to communicate.

The best part of *A Midsummer Night's Dream* for me was getting to know that tremendous Viennese composer, Erich Wolfgang Korngold. He had been brought over by Reinhardt to arrange the Mendelssohn score for the film, and fortunately for Warner Brothers, he was to remain and write scores for some of their best pictures. It happened that Reinhardt had rented Dolores Del Rio's house in Hollywood Hills where he was staying with all his entourage. One day in the studio Dolores walked by, a copper-skinned vision of beauty in crisp white, wearing beautiful red gloves, stunning all the way. Erich, who knew almost no English, turned to me and said, "Cagney!"

"What?"

"Who?" he said, pointing.

"That's Dolores Del Rio."

"Del Rio?" he asked. "Reinhardt house?"

"Yes," I said. His eyes widened and he said incredulously, "Wizzout *her?*"

There was one scene in the film, a process shot, showing the fairies riding moonbeams, and Erich had missed the first screening. On his arrival he was told that he really should go and see this fairy sequence, which he promptly did. When he returned from the viewing room, we all asked, "So, Erich?"

"Ah—*Wunderbar!* Terrific—tremendous—stupendous—but *bad!*"

Right in the middle of shooting *Dream*, our Puck, Mickey Rooney, went up to Big Bear or Arrowhead, got aboard a toboggan, and in descending a slope tried to slow himself down by sticking a leg out. He broke it. Ten days later he was well enough to come back to the set with the leg in a cast, and all subsequent scenes of his were shot from the waist up. For the long shots they used a good double, a boy named George Breakstone, and it worked out satisfactorily.

As Bottom, I simply had another job to do, and I did it. There was no feeling at the time that we were doing anything special, and I think the whole enterprise was a box-office disaster, although since then I believe the picture has taken on an aura of culture. One delightful thing happened during shooting. In the scene where I awaken with the ass's head on, I look in a pond, see myself, and recognize the sad truth. Thereupon I burst into song, all the while weeping copiously. I was rehearsing this when a new shift of stagehands came on the set, and one of them whispered to the chap whose place he was taking, "What's he crying about?"

"He just got a jackass's head."

"Oh, that's what he's cryin' for?"

"Yeah."

"Touchin'."

I followed up *Dream* with *Frisco Kid,* one of those catch-as-catch-can affairs Warner's put out purely because they had to be put out. By that I mean *Frisco Kid* had already been sold to the exhibitors even before a foot of it had been shot or conceived. This will give you some idea of its inherent artistic flavor. The picture was built just the way a Ford sedan might have been.

It was around this time that Will Rogers died, a man I had just gotten to know a bit. A most likable and decent person, he appeared at all the benefits, always with the good routine fully à propos of the occasion. Once I was at a dinner being given for Bill Robinson when Will was master of ceremonies, and I was called on for a word or two. Will introduced me by saying, "Now I'm going to call on someone who, every time I see him work, looks to me like a bunch of firecrackers going off all at once."

I got up and said, "Well, I certainly don't feel like any firecracker or *bunch* of firecrackers at this point. After all that's been said before, I feel like kind of a wet blanket. But I do want to pass on the good wishes for a very happy birthday from a bum hoofer to another." What I had wanted to say was, ". . . from a bum hoofer to a great one!" I was trying to be modest, and in a slip of the tongue I had fouled myself up for fair. At that time I was very

self-conscious at public events. I never had any real poise, any assurance.

It was a great loss when Will Rogers was killed on his 1935
Alaska flight. I remember going into the Green Room at Warner's
the morning we got the news, and a former much-decorated
member of the Lafayette Escadrille was there—Bill Wellman, the
director. I asked him if he had heard the news, and he said,
"Yeah. We just don't belong up there. You couldn't get me into a
plane now for anything." I echo his sentiments about planes. I
hate the damned things myself.

In 1936 I attained one of my best and fondest dreams—I
bought a farm. Martha's Vineyard then was uncluttered with developers (which is too gracious a designation for those gentlemen; developers actually develop nothing but their own
bankrolls). I couldn't think of anything more satisfactory, more
life-fulfilling, than living on a farm surrounded by salt water. This
is what Martha's Vineyard allowed me to do. The old, old house
we found there—its building deed reads 1728—met my expecta-
tions wonderfully, and everything about the land and its situation
charmed me right out of my shoes. Moreover, the taxes were
thirty-nine dollars a year, which made it an ideal place to land if
the movie business ever dropped me. I figured one way or another I could always manage to pick up thirty-nine dollars in the
course of a year. I used to lie in my California bed and dream of
that old house in its very happy state of quiet decay. I loved it
beyond words, and at the time I said to myself, "If I had just six
months to live, I'd spend them at the Vineyard." The Vineyard
represented for me the place where I could always go to find the
freedom and peace one didn't find prevailing on the Hollywood
turf.

By the end of 1935 it became apparent to me and brother Bill
(in his capacity as my business manager) that the studio was still
consistently interested in paying me only a very small percentage
of the income dollar deriving from my work. Therefore I did the
only thing I could do under the circumstances. I walked away

until they could make a better arrangement. We filed suit against Warner's to rectify the inequities.

While waiting for that to straighten itself out, I went to work for Grand National Pictures, a fairly small studio that had been using Warner's for distribution of its product. Here I made a musical, *Something to Sing About,* a particular pleasure to do because it meant working with Harland Dixon and Johnny Boyle, two great dancers I had admired for years in vaudeville. I must cheerfully admit that I had stolen all kinds of steps from them both down through the years, and it made me very proud to think that I was literally following in their footsteps and with their footsteps. It was warming to feel that I was one of their kind—a song-and-dance man working in the great tradition set by the head of our clan, George M. Cohan.

Johnny Boyle became my instructor and very good friend for many of my Hollywood years. He knew more about dancing than anyone I ever met. He could do Irish jigs and reels plus every conceivable kind of buck dance, hard-shoe dance—*any* dance. Personally, Johnny had an awful lot of trouble laughing, and he had reason. He was sent into the mines at age eight as a breaker boy. This meant sitting in a cold, dust-filled room, picking slate out of the coal as it passed under him. Breaker boys were bent over the entire day, and whenever they tried to straighten up, a foreman was always there to force them back with the clout of a shovel. This was Johnny's childhood, and I understood why he tended not to be merry.

Harland Dixon was also a superb dancer and teacher. He was a great dancing innovator, creating such things as shoulder twists and knee snaps, all now standard hoofer techniques. He and Johnny helped considerably in livening up *Something to Sing About.* One time Johnny showed me a pair of miniature gold dancing shoes, and on one sole was engraved: "To Johnny Boyle, the World's Greatest Hoofer; signed, Jack Donohue." This was no faint praise because Jack Donohue had been Marilyn Miller's partner in many Ziegfeld shows and was a musical comedy star of the first rank, a Broadway legend. Johnny was naturally very proud of these gold shoes, and when he showed them to me I noticed that there was nothing inscribed on the other sole. I asked him why Jack had left it blank. "Oh," said Johnny, "that's just in case we'd get an argument from Dixon."

With Johnny's expertise at my beck, I would call on him when I needed to take off some weight before getting into a picture. I'd put on my old sweat clothes and go down to his house. There'd be a dancing mat in the parlor where he'd teach me a routine that I'd employ to sweat my lard off. I had never been taught to dance. As a youngster I'd watch a dance, steal it, change it, usually giving it a little eccentric twist. I was always trying to improve the steps I stole, striving to make them more showy—and Johnny helped me do that. Years before I had done the same thing for my Bill when I put our act together. I would teach her the steps, but then she did them better than I ever thought of doing. Some things I could never do easily—wings, for instance. I never did them well, probably because they didn't pay off; it took an expert to realize how difficult they were. I chose the other route—the more flashy stuff the audience could see—flash, with always a dash of the eccentric and a bit of humor.

Many people think I learned to dance for *Yankee Doodle Dandy,* the prevailing impression being that when a fella gets up and does a dance routine, he learned it the day before yesterday. Not so. A song-and-dance man, which is what I am basically, becomes one over many years of unrelenting work. I'm amazed by reading reports of actors who say, "I'm studying voice and dance now, and I'm going to do a musical comedy next season." Unfailingly, it never happens. To become a dancer, initially you've got to be a little bit off your chump in order to put up with the pain—the sprained ankles, torn tendons, and bumped knees. A person dedicating himself to that kind of hardship needs a particular attitude. I think dancing is a primal urge coming to life at the first moment we need to express joy. Among pre-language aboriginals possessing no music and the most primitive rhythm, I suspect dancing became their first expression of excitement. And an extension of that idea is imbedded in my belief, quite applicable to myself, that once a song-and-dance man, always a song-and-dance man.

After *Something to Sing About,* the difficulty with Warner Brothers was straightened out, and I returned in 1938. The work was all the more pleasant in that two close chums were involved in my first picture on return. They were Pat O'Brien and Ralph Bellamy; the picture was *Boy Meets Girl,* a reworking of the Sam and Bella Spewack hit Broadway farce about the motion picture business. Also in the cast was that very savvy gal, Marie Wilson, who was very adept at giving an impression of naïveté. Like any number of my films, I never saw *Boy Meets Girl.* Years later I saw part of it on television, and it was so much better in the TV version than it seemed to be when we did it that I can't quite understand it. It's the same film, but I sense that the years have done something for it—what, I don't know. While we were making it, Pat and I were harassed by the producer's insistence on more speed. So Pat and I went mostly our own way; we were fast when we needed to be, and let air into it as required for the most part. In a farce you've got to give the audience a chance to get their breath.

Next on the agenda was *Angels with Dirty Faces,* which got some attention at the time but, like so many of the catch-as-catch-can pictures we made then, it had an insubstantial script that the actors patched up here and there by improvising right on the set. In *Angels,* for instance, one of the first scenes has Pat O'Brien as the priest in the confessional, and I as Rocky the hood on the other side of the covered window. In the script as written, the priest slides back the latticed opening and says, "What can I do for you, my son?" Then I am supposed to say, "What did you do with those fountain pens we stole out of the freight car fifteen years ago?" The priest says, "Rocky!," and we shake hands. This was ludicrous. Pat and I, raised in the Church, knew the ceremonial forms, and very well did we know them. As it happened, on this picture the director, the producer, and the writer were all Jewish, so how could they be expected to know? I said to the director, Mike Curtiz, "Mike, you can't do the scene as written."

He asked why and I said, "There is a certain ritual to confession, and the ritual must be observed. The priest doesn't say, 'What can I do for you, my son?' First, the penitent says, 'Bless me, father, for I have sinned. I confess to Almighty God and to you, father. My last confession was thus-and-so many weeks ago, et cetera, et cetera.' That's just for *openers*. Then after it's all over, the priest gives the penitent some penance. And there's no hand-shaking, believe me!" Mike said, "Well, couldn't they walk *outside* and shake hands?" So Pat and I fashioned the scene as it needed to be.

By this time in my career, what with my experiences in the other pictures featuring gunfire going slightly awry, one would think I'd learned my lesson. But here I was in *Angels with Dirty Faces* facing the real thing again. I was up at a window firing down at the police, and one shot called for me to be right at the opening as machine-gun bullets took the window out around my head. Then, whatever it was—common sense or a hunch—something made me cautious, and I said to Mike Curtiz, "Do it in process." (That was basically a superimposition.)

"Jim, this man will not hurt you."

"Do it in process, Mike. I will not be there." I got out of the scene, and Burke, the professional machine gunner, fired the shots. One of the bullets hit the steel edge of the window, was deflected, and went right through the wall where my head had been. That convinced me, need I say it, that flirting this way with real bullets was ridiculous.

The character I played in the picture, Rocky Sullivan, was in part modeled on a fella I used to see when I was a kid. He was a hophead and a pimp, with four girls in his string. He worked out of a Hungarian rathskeller on First Avenue between Seventy-seventh and Seventy-eighth streets—a tall dude with an expensive straw hat and an electric-blue suit. All day long he would stand on that corner, hitch up his trousers, twist his neck and move his necktie, lift his shoulders, snap his fingers, then bring his hands together in a soft smack. His invariable greeting was "Whadda ya hear? Whadda ya say?" The capacity for observation is something every actor must have to some degree, so I recalled this fella and his mannerisms, and gave them to Rocky Sullivan just to bring some modicum of difference to this roughneck. I did that gesturing maybe six times in the picture—that was over thirty years ago —and the impressionists are still doing me doing *him*.

The Cagney mimics I've seen lately, however, don't hitch the trousers so much as just put their hands out in front and kind of wag their heads a bit, and I think they've lost something. One item a number of them do get right is the one of holding my arms in front of my thighs instead of at the side, as most people do. This is my natural stance, due to my having done a great deal of weight lifting from boyhood on. Indeed, I have done so much lifting and hard work through the years that I can't straighten my arms. My tendons have actually shortened. I don't try to hold my arms in any particular way, they just hang there in front, completely relaxed.

Most of my imitators also say, "All right, you guys!," which I don't remember ever saying. I think some of these modifications of Rocky came from the Bowery Boys grabbing some of those mannerisms and altering them slightly when they made their own series. Their constant repetition of those altered mannerisms might have influenced the professional imitators because, for instance, "All right, you guys!" sounds like a Bowery Boys' line to me. Moreover, I *never* said, "You dirty rat!"

The Bowery Boys, known as the Dead End Kids when we made *Angels with Dirty Faces* in 1938, had been throwing their weight around quite a bit with directors and other actors at the time. It developed that I was to have a little off-screen encounter with them. Our opening scene in the picture takes place in the basement of a deserted building. I am fresh out of Sing Sing, and the kids have just rolled me for my wallet. I walk in, tell them to hand over, and with a little emphatic coercion force them to get up the wallet. According to the script my next line was "Come here, suckers," and I lead them over to the door on which is carved "Rocky Sullivan," put there when I was a kid. The kids must look at this with respectful awe because of my rough reputation and say, "*You're* Rocky Sullivan?"

We shot the scene, but just before I said, "Come here, suckers," Leo Gorcey said, "He's psychic!," thereby throwing the rhythm of the scene right out the window, souring the whole thing very nicely. So in the next take just before I said, "Come here, suckers," I gave Leo Gorcey a stiff arm right above the nose —bang! His head went back, hitting the kid behind him, stunning them both momentarily. Then I said, "Now listen here, we've got some work to do, so let's have none of this goddamned nonsense. When we get on, we're pros—we're doing the job we're asked to do. Understood?"

"Yeah," they said. One of the kids turned to Gorcey and said, "Who the hell you think you got there—Bogart?" I learned later that Bogie had incurred their disfavor on a film they'd done together, and they expressed their displeasure by taking his pants off. But in our picture, once they had learned that their jumping me would be troublesome for them, we got along fine.

The leading lady of *Angels with Dirty Faces* was that lovely, talented gal, Ann Sheridan. So much to offer—and a three-pack-a-day smoker. She just didn't eat because cigarettes killed her appetite. One day a well-known doctor came on the *Angels* set, and after we got talking a bit, I asked him to lunch, inviting Annie to join us. At the table she lit a cigarette immediately. She ordered ham and eggs, took one little bit of the ham, then lit another cigarette. The doctor asked her if she smoked a great deal and she said, "Oh, yes." He said, "And you don't eat." Annie said she just didn't feel like eating at the moment. The doctor said, "You know, time was when coronary thrombosis was a great new thing among women. Whenever it happened, it went up and down the land, doctor to doctor—'a female coronary!' Not lately. Cigarettes have done it." Annie said, "Oh, really?" and went right on smoking. Years later when the lung cancer hit, she didn't have much of a chance, and what a powerful shame that was. A mighty nice gal, Annie.

The ending of *Angels with Dirty Faces* has prompted a continually asked question over the years: did Rocky turn yellow as he walked to the electric chair, or did he just pretend to? For those who haven't seen the picture, I must explain that Rocky becomes the idol of the street kids in his old neighborhood, and when he is ultimately brought to justice and condemned to die, these youngsters still hold him up as a model to emulate. Rocky's childhood pal, now a priest, comes to him in the death house and pleads with him to kill the kids' unhealthy admiration of him by turning yellow at the last minute, by pretending cowardice as he is being led to the electric chair. Rocky scorns the request.

The execution scene is this: cheekily contemptuous of my escorts, I am being led along the last mile when suddenly, without any warning, I go into a seizure of fear, twisting and turning in the clutch of the guards as I try to prevent them from leading me into the death chamber. Or *is* it a seizure of fear? Am I not instead doing a favor for my priest pal and the kids by pretending to be yellow, thereby discouraging the youngsters from following in my convict footsteps? Through the years I have actually had little kids come up to me on the street and ask, "Didya do it for the father, huh?" I think in looking at the film it is virtually impossible to say which course Rocky took—which is just the way I wanted it. I played it with deliberate ambiguity so that the spectator can take his choice. It seems to me it works out fine in either case. You have to decide.

It was this picture and others like it, of course, that guaranteed me a tough-guy image, an image that I am bound to say has sometimes proved mighty wearisome to me off the screen. People who don't know me have asked friends if I was really a tough character, and upon receiving assurance that I was just doing a job when portraying a hood, have perhaps not always been convinced. One fella at Warner's with a very real ability to inject himself into any conversation, had a question for me one time. "Off-screen," he said, "you're very quiet and unassuming, but when you get on there, you're a pretty boisterous fella." I admitted this. His memorable comeback was, "Now, when are you acting—on-screen, or off?"

The confusion of the individual with the role he plays can cause the backyard weight lifter to decide that he can easily take the movie tough guy, and these challengers appear at the damnedest times. Years and years ago I was at the Cocoanut Grove for a New Year's gathering, seated at a table with my back to the dance floor, chatting with my friends. A complete stranger slapped me on the back and demanded to know how I was. This is one thing that really burns me, so I paid no attention. A bit later he came around again and said, "Why don't you get up and dance, Jimmy? Come on, have some fun—you're too quiet." I told the people I was with, "I've got to get out of here or I'm going to take this son-of-a-bitch." They saw trouble brewing so we got up to go, reached the door, and Mr. Loudmouth actually came after me.

"Oh, what's the matter, Jimmy, can't you take it?" he said.

"Oh, you son-of-a-bitch," I said, and started for him. Fortunately two talent agents I knew grabbed my arms and pulled me away because I was primed to beat the bejesus out of that character.

A similar clown confronted me when Jack MacCaulay, an old Columbia school chum of mine, and I went up to see Dartmouth play Yale. During the half, three or four typical college lads with the crewcuts and flowing neck mufflers came over to me. They offered a drink, and when I declined with thanks, they asked if I drank, and I said no. Their ringleader was standing on the long concrete steps leading down to the field, and he regarded me with some truculence. After learning that I didn't drink, he offered me a cigarette, which I also politely refused. "Look," he said, "we're going to a party right after the game and we'd like you to come with us." I explained that I was committed to going up north right after the game.

"Ohhh—and you don't drink?" I said no. "And you don't smoke?" I said no. "And you won't come to the party?" I said no.

"Well, maybe you'd like to fight?"

"What a horse's ass you are," I said. "Starting an argument with your back turned to thirty feet of concrete steps. What do you suppose would happen with one belt?"

"Oh, yeah—like that, huh?"

"Yeah."

"O.K.," he said, and walked away.

My reaction in these instances has inevitably been to do the thing I was raised to do: cheerfully belt the guy who gets out of line. But that doesn't work these days, and I've decided that the only thing to do is to stay out of public places where these clowns foregather. The average person out for a social evening is on his best behavior, but among them is usually a single jackass who has to make the splurge. And if I hit one of these creeps, who would have been wrong? Who would have received all the publicity?

And yet I should be grateful that my tough-guy image is something I could put on at will. Too many of the lads in my old neighborhood were unable to remove that image because it was engrained. Like Bootah, my old classmate who really did go to death row, and Willie Carney, the boy I had the three-day fight with. Some time after I had been in pictures, I heard from Willie. He had served time for robbery, and while in prison had terrorized all the guards right up to the head keeper. Willie was transferred from Sing Sing to Dannemora, a hellhole for incorrigibles. While there, the story had it, he cut another prisoner's throat and was consigned to Pilgrim State Hospital for the Criminally Insane on Long Island.

While there he wrote me. I've still got that letter. It reads, "Dear Jim, Maybe you remember when you and me hooked it up on Seventy-second Street and First Avenue. I'm over here at the Pilgrim State Hospital. My nerves are all shot, but I'm going to get out next spring. My sister is going to take care of me. If you have any old clothes you're not using, I'd appreciate your sending them on. Cigarettes, anything."

Of course I sent him clothing, cigarettes, and money, unfortunately putting the last item in cash. I never heard from Willie again. The best guess as to what happened is that the kindly guards glommed onto all of it. His life was such a waste because he had a talent for leadership. All the kids in the block were in great awe of him, and even the grownups kept a respectful distance. His parents were both on the bottle, and his older brother, Danny, tried to substitute for them. But the streets of New York were too tough even for a guy as tough as Willie.

～ 5 ～

By the late 1930s, my pattern of living was fairly well set. Learn the words, do the scenes, and then when the picture was finished, without any delay, back East to Martha's Vineyard. On the final day's shooting, I'd hector the assistant director a bit by asking him if this really was the last day, if I could absolutely count on being free tomorrow for departure. And when it was certain that I was, on the phone immediately to reserve a drawing room for the following morning.

When we moved to Martha's Vineyard, I didn't understand the Vineyarders. Or more specifically, I couldn't understand why they were so distant, so obviously resentful of off-islanders. I would say good morning to them, and they deep-froze me, going right on by. Gradually I began to understand. First, of course, I was an off-islander, and, second, I was an actor. I might as well have had three heads. At that time I wrote:

> When you give your heart to fair Martha's Isle
> That Queen of insular sluts,
> It's like falling in love with a beautiful whore
> Who hates your goddamned guts.

Once a group of newspapermen and cameramen was coming to the island to do a story on me. This was late November and a very harsh November, too, when boats were irregularly scheduled. On the scheduled date the boat didn't come, and the Warner's publicity man asked me to please make it to Woods

Hole over on the mainland. I asked a farmer who worked for me just how I could charter a boat, and he arranged for Frankie Vincent to take me over. On the way over in the darkness, Frankie Vincent began to talk about the farmer who had arranged the charter. He learned from me that the farmer was MacInnis, from "up-island"—the west side of the island.

"Oh," said Frankie, "the son of MacInnis, the jeweler downtown. I understand he works for an actor fella up-island." I admitted that, I admitted I was the actor. "Oh, good God almighty!," said Frankie, "you never know who you're going to meet, do you?" I told Frankie I had found an old genealogy in my attic tracing the Vincents back in all their full chronology to 1765. He said these were his people. I said I presumed that they might be, and I asked him if he ever got up our way, to Chilmark. "Oh, no," he said, "last time I was up that way was fifteen—twenty years ago." Chilmark is eight miles away.

A mighty pleasant old fella, Frankie, and we got along fine. The next time I saw him he was over at Woods Hole, and I said, "Hello, Mr. Vincent."

"Hello, Mr. Cagney."

"I enjoyed my trip with you," I said.

"I did, too. It was very entertaining for me 'cause we don't meet very many people like you."

Not long after that, I ran into him again, and he said, "You know, it's a very interesting thing—but everybody says you're kind of a snotty guy. That's what they say. I haven't found you that way."

"Mr. Vincent," I said, "let me explain. I came to the island because it's quiet and remote from all the things I'm used to. And when people come into my backyard and drive busloads of tourists in there, *that's* when I get really snotty and say mean things. The bus driver complains of my snottiness. Well, he simply demands the privilege of coming into my property with his big bus loaded with people clicking cameras, full of questions, when all I want is a bit of quiet and the privacy any person is absolutely entitled to."

During those early years at the Vineyard our front yard, about a ten-acre piece, had become badly overgrown, so Mr. MacInnis thought of Gilson Hammett, a farmer next door, who owned a mowing machine. Mac walked over to Hammett's, talked with him, and it was all arranged. I left the island for a few days, and on return I noticed that the cutting had not been done. Mac walked over to Hammett's and asked him why nothing had happened.

"Well," said Hammett, "I got there to do it with my horse and the mowing machine, and there was a sign on the gate that said 'No Admittance—Trespassers Punished.' So I turned around and came on home."

"That didn't mean *you*—!" Mac said to him.

"It didn't *say* that," said Hammett. Remarkable people—people of their word.

It has been very interesting to see how protective the Vineyarders gradually became of the actor fella. Although I didn't know them, never met them, whenever any of the islanders were asked by tourists where I lived, they were never told. One tourist walked into a real country store in North Tisbury about five miles from me and said, "How do I get to Cagney's house?"

"What do you want to know for?" said little Maude Call from behind the counter.

"I'd like to see him."

"Do you know him?"

"No."

"Why do you want to see him?"

"I'd like to talk to him."

"About what?"

"Well—" He wasn't very sure.

"Look," said Maude, "if you don't know him, don't bother him. Let him alone. The poor man is trying to get a little peace and quiet, and you damned fools are always rushing into his house and asking silly questions. Now, stay away from him!" This kind of protective response from Vineyarders to inquiring strangers has happened a number of times, and I am much appreciative.

The most amusing incident of the period when I was new to the island happened when we were staying with some friends, the Wortmans, at Chilmark. Also staying at the Wortmans' was my old pal, that tremendous singer, actor, and all-round big broth of a boy, Ed McNamara. Ed took a chair, sat out front, and when people would drive in and ask where Cagney was, he'd reply, "Tell you what to do. There's a man named Ellison Hoover, a very, very interesting man himself, and he's entertaining the Cagneys. You go right down there now and see him." Mac would give precise instructions on how to get to Hoover's house.

Now, Ellison Hoover was about as close as one can come to the definition of misanthrope. Except for a few close friends (and we counted ourselves among them), he wanted nobody around at all. On this occasion Mac kept sending people down to Hoover's for a goodly number of days. Then, intensely curious, Mac, Wortman, and I drove down to Hoover, whom we hadn't seen for a week or so, and when we got to his house we saw all the shades drawn, everything quiet as a tomb. We knocked on the door. No answer. Then we proceeded to holler, "Ellison! Ellison! Ellison Hoover!"

Finally an upstairs window shade was pushed aside, and we saw that jaundiced, rheumy blue eye of Ellison's peeking out. He stormed downstairs and flew at us. "You sonsabitches," he thundered. "I haven't had a minute's peace in a week. Goddamn you!" What we had actually done was to confirm for Ellis his overall opinion of the worth of the human race.

Ellison, a fine artist, attained a kind of fame ultimately. When Clare Briggs died and his cartoon strip, "Mr. and Mrs.," needed an artist, the New York *Tribune* signed up Ellison. Art Farwell did the script and Ellison the cartooning. On the side Ellison executed magnificent crayon drawings, beautiful things that he didn't regard highly, doing them only for his friends. He was quite a guy, and I was very fond of him. Along the way in show business I had picked up some broken-down Dutch comedy bits, and these would paralyze Ellison. For example, the Dutch burlesque comedian would alter "by a curious coincidence" to "by a curious coinkidinkie," and Ellison would fall down laughing. His reaction to these phrases reminds me of a Dutch comic's phrase that Frank McHugh always used—"Hello, cheesy—Hello, cheesy." I knew there had to be some kind of burlesque background to that, so I asked Frank to fill me in. Frank explained all he knew of it was that after the burlesque comedian is on stage, a phone would ring, he'd make all kinds of elaborate approaches to it, finally picking it up to say, "Helllooo, Hello! I want to speak to the Cheese of Polize, please. . . . Ooooohhh, Hello, Cheesy!" And that was all Frank remembered of the routine. I knew there had to be an ending to it somewhere, and I kept asking around to no avail. Finally I learned the end of the routine from that fine actor, Jim Barton.

Jim knew all the burlesque bits, and when I asked him if he knew the "Hello, Cheesy" thing, he said he certainly did. The burlesque comedian goes to the phone and asks for the "Cheese of Polize, please. . . . Ooohh, hellooo, Cheesy. I didn't recockognize your voice. Cheesy, I got me here a delheminna. A very, very zerious delheminna. . . . Oh? Hmm? Not 'delheminna'? Oh— 'probablem'? All right, I got me here a probablem. Cheesy, by a curious coinkidinkie, I godt me here all dis carpet. Dere's carpet on the floor, dere's carpet on the vindows, dere's carpet on the valls, dere's carpet on the zeeling, dere's carpet *everywhere!* Now —vot I vonder, Cheesy, is dis—vot do I *do* with all dis carpet? . . . Mmmm? . . . Oooohhhhh, Cheesy! *ALL* dis carpet?"

And speaking of a burlesque, there is the little matter of *The Oklahoma Kid,* made in 1939, which was my first Western. A Western is something not as foreign to a former New York street kid as one might think. I am, have been, and will be always a man for horses. There are many beautiful sights in this beautiful world, but I really cannot think that there is anything to equal a pair of superb Morgans—or any other horses, for that matter—standing proud and straight in all their beauty on a well-turfed field. As horse opera, *The Oklahoma Kid* is a typical example of how the motion picture business too many times takes the easiest way creatively. The picture was an idea of Ted Paramore's, who conceived of doing the story of the mountain men, particularly of their paragon, Kit Carson. We researched it and I came up with some things I wanted to do, pretty exciting things, I thought. Warner's, without warning pulled Paramore off the script and without a word to me, changed directors. When I got the final script it had as much to do with actual history as the Katzenjammer Kids. It had become typical horse opera, just another programmer.

The clothing I had elected to wear—worn shirt and pants, broken-down hat—was replaced by the fanciest kind of cowboy costume. The script was so typically predictable that again the actors were reduced to cuffing it, ad-libbing where we thought it would do the most good. Not long ago I was at a party and a gentleman there said he had seen me on television in the "feel the air" movie. Funny how little things you drop in a picture can become the most memorable things about it for most people. This bit of business derived from a friend of Ed McNamara's, a gent who had the habit of inhaling deeply when going outdoors, saying, "Feel that air, just *feel* it!," and proceeding to do so. Simply to give my one-dimensional character in *The Oklahoma Kid* something just a trifle memorable, I dropped this little bit in several times—reaching up to feel the air as I said that line—and it persisted in audience memory.

At one point in the film, standing on a rock while a bunch of bad guys led by Bogie and Ward Bond pound by on their horses, I was supposed to launch a lariat at Ward's horse, get it snugly around the neck, and pull it up short. Naturally, such a trick roping is done by an expert while they show the hands of the rope artist, then shoot a closeup of me straining and heaving.

But on this occasion I was intrigued by the thought of handling a rope, so I went over to the wrangler scheduled to do the actual roping and asked him just how he did it. He asked me if I had ever roped before, and I told him honestly I never had. Whereupon he showed me the looping and the general mechanics

15. In another of his eight films with Pat O'Brien. *Angels with Dirty Faces,* 1938.

16. A trio distinctly up to no good. With Frank McHugh and Humphrey Bogart, *The Roaring Twenties,* 1939.

17. "Bill" and Jim with Casey and young Jim.

18. Facing the battling Cagney is Frank McHugh; above and to the right, Donald Crisp and George Tobias. *City for Conquest*, 1941.

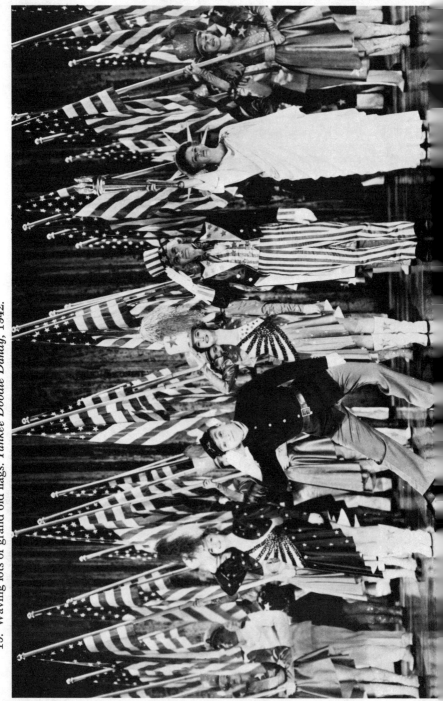

19. Waving lots of grand old flags. *Yankee Doodle Dandy,* 1942.

of the procedure, and I thought just for the hell of it I'd try the trick myself, never dreaming for a moment that it would work.

It worked. As Bogie and Ward came in on the shot riding their horses past my rock, I threw that loop button-bright right over the neck of Ward's horse. I held on to the rope for just a brief second, then let go—otherwise I'd have taken Ward right off his perch. The director, Lloyd Bacon, yelled "Cut!"

"Why didn't you hang on?" Lloyd asked me.

"What did you want me to do—kill Ward?"

Lloyd said merrily, "Why not?"

So the shot turned out to be effective. The wrangler who showed me the basics came over to me and said very skeptically, "So you never threw a rope before?"

"So help me, never did."

"Uh-huh," he said. "Isn't that great?" He walked away, the picture of total disbelief. Every time I saw him thereafter he looked at me and said, "So you never threw a rope before?"

Outside of the little extra bits and pieces dropped in by the actors, everything about *The Oklahoma Kid* was cliché, even the ending—guy getting gal, kiss, fadeout. So I thought a bit about how to spruce it up. What I finally did was to construct a little sequence beginning with the moment the girl's father (Donald Crisp) says "Congratulations" to me for winning her. Instead of going into the clinch then as per the script, I looked at him, looked at her, looked at her again, took off my hat, handed it to Donald, and said, "Hold that." Clinch and fadeout. A minor thing, but it removed the heavy hand of banality weighing down that ending. After he saw it, that very good director, Lewis "Millie" Milestone, nodded approvingly and said, "I was wondering how you were going to get out of that one."

Banal script notwithstanding, the actors went to the post set to do the best job we could with the material at hand. Bogie played a heavy in it, doing his usual expert job. By this time in his career he'd become entirely disillusioned with the picture business. Endlessly the studio required him to show up without his even knowing what the script was, what his dialogue was, what the picture was about. On top of this he would be doing two or three pictures at a time. That's how much they appreciated him.

He came into the makeup department one morning and I said, "What is it today, Bogie?" "Oh, I don't know," he said. "I was told to go over to Stage 12." There he was fulfilling his contract, doing as required, however much against his will. We shared the same attitude: when there's a job to be done, you do it. New acting talent would come along, and the studio's idea of building them up was simply to throw them into one picture after another as quickly as possible. In this sink-or-swim situation the ones who survived were the ones with natural durability. Bogie had that kind of durability. Albeit he was a tremendous personality, the studio didn't do anything about him until fortuitous circumstances put him opposite Ingrid Bergman in *Casablanca,* and away went Bogie. Sheer accident. The studio had no thought of using him to the fullest, indeed of using *anyone* to the fullest bent of their talent. The policy toward talent was simplistic: just throw them in, then throw them out. Talent was not nurtured, it was simply consumed.

Another durable fella was George Raft, who did *Each Dawn I Die* with me. With typical confusion, Warner's had somebody else ticketed to play the part I finally played, a reporter railroaded to prison; and George wound up playing the hoodlum role, instead of the usual other way around. George was a real pro, letter-perfect in his lines every day, every word. I must say I can't say the same for myself.

When we were doing *Each Dawn I Die,* Freddie Astaire came over to have lunch with us. Freddie had been in the big Dillingham shows in New York around the time George was playing nightclubs there. That was how they got to know each other, and Freddie had a great regard for George as a dancer and, of course, vice versa. It was interesting to watch their meeting after all those years. Both of these very sensitive fellas were shy of each other, keenly self-conscious. I realized at once that very little would be said unless I jumped in and played straight man for them. I did so gladly. Finally George unwound and began telling some vividly interesting stories about his mother and himself in their early days of privation.

When he was fifteen and his mother in her early thirties, they used to enter flatfoot waltz contests in the hopes of getting the five-dollar prize. In a flatfoot waltz you cannot take your heels off the floor, forcing you to glide over it as if it were a magnet. George used to cut holes in his heels and insert dimes so that the gliding would be easier. He and his mother did very well on the dance-hall circuit, and later on when he got into the nightclubs, he did a very fast and a very good eccentric Charleston.

George told Freddie and me that in those early days he used piano wire for shoelaces. He laced them up tightly in order to numb his feet so he could dance faster. I told him that was dangerous as hell to do, and he agreed. "I know," he said, "I found out later. I used to get pale green around the mouth. I was actually suffering a mild heart attack." George also told us that when he was working for the clubs, he was really working for the Mob—capital M. They, of course, owned all the New York nightclubs, and were expanding into Florida. In a single night in New York, George would work as many as seven nightclubs, going from one to the other, repeating his very strenuous act in each establishment. Finally he got into a Dillingham show on Broadway that became the climax of his career to that date, and the clubs became of secondary importance.

The Mob, however, had different ideas. They told George he was going to Florida to open their new nightclub down there. George explained that he couldn't because of the Dillingham show, but the tough boys weren't having any of that. He raised hell, said he couldn't do it, but did agree to go down to the train that night to see the boys off for Florida. At the station they grabbed him, took off his overcoat, shoes, and hat—and hid them. "All right," George said, "you win!" He got on the train. But as they pulled into North Philadelphia, he jumped off and ran in his stocking feet through the snow to catch a taxi back to New York. He made the Dillingham show that night and didn't show up in Florida as planned.

Somebody else who assumed that George's natural gentleness made him an easy mark was Peter Lorre. Lorre felt greatly superior to George, regarding him as a lowbrow. In a picture they were doing together, Lorre said in his inimitable whine, "Georgie, here's what you do. You come over here—," and he took George by the arm to guide him. But you don't take George Raft by the arm and do *anything*. You can suggest something, but you do not guide him, you do *not* push him. George said very pleasantly to Lorre, "Don't take my arm. Just tell me what you've got in mind." Lorre began to explain and took George's arm again. George told him not to do that, and once more Lorre took forceful charge, and *bang!* Lorre got smacked right between the eyes, knocking him ass over teakettle. Then George said very nicely, "I told you not to do that." Mr. Lorre didn't do it again. And Georgie has survived piano wire laces, Mr. Lorre, and the New York Mob, thank you very much, and is now close to eighty, still in fine fettle. A very nice guy.

George Raft was typical of the interesting breed of actors I worked with at Warner's. They were a lively bunch, and one of the liveliest was Allen Jenkins. In the early days he was rather an undisciplined fella. One time when he was very unhappy with the way the studio was treating him, he got drunk and called up Darryl Zanuck, very hard-driving and able man that he was, and told Zanuck what he could do with the contract. At the time Allen made this phone call, Pat O'Brien was in the room with him. Pat was just starting a brand-new contract at about four grand a week on a forty-week basis, a tidy sum. Allen went into full gear with his tirade against Zanuck, topping it off with, "Now you can take your contract and shove it, and that goes for O'Brien, too!" Pat shouted, "Leave me out of it!" Nothing happened as a consequence. Jenkins went back to work because Zanuck knew him as a tempestuous personality who cherished a drink or two. That was the old Allen. Before his death recently he had gone absolutely AA for a number of years.

Another Warner's regular was George Tobias, and I had a particular affection for George because he was an open and direct kind of fella—the kind of man one could describe with total accuracy as *nice*. George played a French Canuck in one of the pictures, and as we sat at a table rehearsing the lines, I noticed that one of his pronunciations was not authentic. I asked him if I might make a suggestion, and he readily agreed. I explained that his way of saying so-and-so was inaccurate. "You're not kidding me now?" he said, knowing that gags and leg-pulling were standard operations in our coterie. I assured him I wasn't, and he promptly said he would speak the line the way I pronounced it. I spoke it for him, and he agreed that it sounded correct. During the shot he pronounced it that way, and it all worked out very well. This was so typical of George—an openness and a warm directness that made working with him such a comfortable experience.

The best part of the entire Warner Brothers setup was this stock company—guys and gals who knew their business, did the job, and had fun doing it. As to the material we had to work with, we set no great store by it because the boys turning out scripts were doing the best they could under the perpetual rush-rush conditions. Writers were pressed to crank out their stuff by the yard, and consequently there was a limited story line in all their things. These pictures became what I've already labeled "cuff operas," which went to the camera as the actors did a "You say this to me and then I'll say that to you" structuring.

An excellent example of that was the first day of shooting *The Roaring Twenties*. Our director, Raoul Walsh, asked me how I liked the opening scene as written, and I said I thought it was pretty bad, as indeed it was. "I think so, too," Raoul said, "I've got a new one. Want to hear it?" I told him to fire away, and after he finished telling it, I told him the one I had in mind. Then Frank McHugh said he had one, so Raoul and I listened to Frank's, and by the end of his description, Raoul and I said, "There it is!" So we shot Frank's, and one hell of a good opening it was. Those pictures were sheer product, and if anyone was practicing art, I never saw it.

So while we were on the set of *The Roaring Twenties,* we made changes constantly, hoping to bring life to the silly thing. A case in point. In a gangster film there is no cliché so strident as one guy knocking another out. In the script two hoods come up to me, one says something that prompts me to bounce him, and down he goes. I varied the scene by placing the second hood behind the first, and when I belted No. 1 his head went back, hit No. 2 in the chin, and they both went down.

This dropping in of the little touches became engrained. You'd frequently go back to your own memories to find these things, as I've said, and at one spot in *The Roaring Twenties* a funny bit derived from a true story I had been told years before. There was a studio worker who bragged to his pals about the great girl he had: "Fellas, wait'll you see her. She's the most beautiful thing you ever saw, and she's crazy about me. You don't *know* the thing we have." Minutes later with his pals still around him, he calls his girl. "Hello, dear. . . . Huh? This is Frankie. *Frankie.* . . . Oh, huh. Huh. . . . How about dinner tonight? . . . No? Well, can I come over *after* dinner? . . . Oh, your mother. Yeah, I see. Well, I'll just pop in for a second on my way home from the studio. . . . Huh? Oh, I see. Well, I'll tell you what. When I'm driving by, can I honk my horn?"

This actually happened, and I dropped it right into *The Roaring Twenties.* According to the script I have to go backstage to talk with Priscilla Lane, now a great success in show business while I have remained an old friend in the small time. I am asking her out to dinner and she has to turn me down. So I simply followed the basic dialogue as uttered by that studio worker years before, concluding with, "Is it all right if I blow my horn as I go by?" Just another bit of flavor to a bland piece of writing.

Of course, when the substance is there, it is a pleasure to do your job and work for a richer kind of creativity. Then the performer has to translate into action the author's intention. How well he does that establishes his worth as an actor. I've seen hit New York shows with top actors; I've seen the same show in Los Angeles with a road company, and the whole worth and impact of the show has been reduced by 50 per cent. Somehow the second-ary cast has not projected the author's intention.

I believe strongly that this is one thing basic to our business—the intention of the author must be clear. You walk out on the stage intending to project to the audience the idea the writer had in mind, and if you don't, the whole point, obviously, is lost or mislaid. Ed McNamara was a pupil of Enrico Caruso; indeed, he was Caruso's *only* pupil. The first thing Caruso said when Mac came to study with him was, "First, Ed, you gotta to have the *in-tention.* You have the intention, and then you stay witha the in-tention, and you-a never for a moment let it get away from you. Because if you-a do, the picture is muddy, the intention is lost, and the audience doesn't get what you mean for-a them to have."

When Mac first went to Caruso, he did so as the result of a frameup. A pal of his, Senator Billy Hughes of New Jersey, went to Caruso and said, "O.K., you guinea, you think you can sing? We got a boy over in Paterson who makes you sound like a she-mouse's poop." Caruso had to hear this prodigy obviously, so Billy got Ed up to the Ansonia Hotel where Caruso lived on the pretext that they were going to meet some old pals. When he saw Ca-ruso opening the hotel room door, Mac damned near fainted, but he got his Irish up because he knew there'd been a plot of some kind. Caruso said he heard that Ed sang and sang "good." Ed ad-mitted this, and in reply to Caruso's request that he sing some-thing, defiantly picked Caruso's greatest number, "Vesti la giubba." Ed gave it everything, rattling the windows, and Caruso enjoyed it very much, asking him to do it again with everything he had. Ed thought he had given everything he had, but he did it once more, almost giving himself a double hernia as he pow-erhoused along. Caruso thought it was great and then pleaded with Ed to do it just *once* more, and again with everything in his power. Ed gave it everything he had, tearing the whole room apart virtually. When he finished, Caruso said, "That's-a fine!" casually, and started to walk away. Mac grabbed Caruso's coattail and said, "Hey, just a minute. Why did you make me do that the third time?"

"I just want-a see you break-a you goddamned neck!" said Caruso.

But Caruso was so impressed with this voice—he called it the finest natural organ he'd ever heard—that he insisted Mac study. Mac, who'd never had a lesson in his life, asked for the name of a good teacher, and Caruso, fearing the charlatan instructors all over the city, had Mac come and work with him. So Mac would come over to the Ansonia, always at nine in the morning, and invariably with the windows wide open in all kinds of weather. He discovered why Caruso set it up this way when one morning a voice bellowed from two flights up, reviling them royally. This was the great singer and rival of Caruso, Titta Ruffo, who lived in the Ansonia too. Ruffo stuck his head out of his window and yelled down, "You son-of-a-bitch, you bastards. I'm-a trying to sleep up-a here." Caruso stuck his head out the window and knowing damned well he was bugging Ruffo, cautioned him, "Shhh!! Great-a singer here, great-a singer."

Caruso was pre-eminently an artist who carried intention to its fullest extensions. He said to Mac, "To sing-a sad, you gotta feel-a sad, really sad. You feel-a happy, then sing-a happy, but unless you feel-a happy, you cannot sing with the intention." This is as may be for those who can do it that way, but speaking purely for myself, I believe all an actor has to do is know the intention, understand the emotion to the fullest, and then call the doing of it into service. The adherents of the so-called Method insist that an actor has to *be* the part. *Be* it. May I say politely, "bunk!" I don't hold with the Method because I've seen it get in the way. These actors so frequently perform not for the audience, but for themselves. This to me is heresy. It is, after all, for the people in the audience that you exist as an actor. It is for them that you perform. Indeed, to repeat with emphasis, audiences determine the material itself.

As verification of that, there is the account of Frank Fay and his bookings. Frank had been playing for weeks at the Palace in New York as a headliner, and on the Monday matinee when all the booking agents gathered to look at the week's new acts with a thought to booking them in theatres across the country, one out-of-town agent was heard to say about Frank, "Such a great talent, but I wouldn't dream of hiring him for my theatres." What he meant was that the sophisticated Fay material simply wouldn't play in vaudeville houses outside New York and the big cities.

Certainly Warner Brothers usually had a pretty good idea of what the public wanted, no matter how derelict they were in helping the material get fashioned. They took advantage of the nostalgia for World War I with *The Fighting 69th*, the great Irish regiment from New York. What with all the Micks in the stock company, it did seem a natural. There were Pat O'Brien, Frank McHugh, Alan Hale, George Brent, and Tommy Dugan. Most people who know the movies will remember Tommy as the frozen-faced comedian who invariably played company managers or old vaudevillians. Indeed, he was an old vaudevillian, one of the first deadpan comedians that I can remember. He was a very funny man, never laughed, but sure made everybody else do so.

We were doing some night shots for *The Fighting 69th* on the Warner ranch, and some coffee seemed like a good idea. Tommy volunteered to do this because he was an expert coffee-maker, so he started to gather wood, and Frank McHugh volunteered to help him. Frank helped him and helped him and helped him to a point where Tommy never got the coffee on the fire because he didn't even get the fire made. It was a scene they should have put in the picture. Finally, coffee was brought in from outside, and at midnight we got the box lunches traditional for location work. Tommy was chewing on a piece of chicken, and a bone got stuck crosswise in his throat. He thought he'd get rid of it by pouring down some hot coffee. It was hot all right, so hot it scalded him severely all the way down, and he was on his way to the hospital in very short order. But he came out of it with comparative ease.

Hardly anything disturbed Tommy; that deadpan never altered. Yet one day I actually saw him smile, and I was amazed. Solid, tough, good stuff, Tommy. Once he was driving on the perimeter of Los Angeles and picked up three hitchhiking servicemen. He took them some way, then courteously explained that this was as far as he was going in their direction. One of the soldiers said belligerently, "Look, mister. You take us all the way to where we're going—or else," or words to that effect. Now, Tommy was well up in his sixties, but he stopped the car carefully, put on the brake, went around, and opened the door. Then he said, "Out, punks. I'll take you on one at a time." And he would have too if they hadn't chickened. Pure spunk.

Moreover, Tommy had a discerning eye. During the making of the picture he said to me, "You don't seem to have had much comfort out of this fame that you should have been enjoying all these years, Jim." I told him there has been no comfort at all in the sheer fact of celebrityhood, none at all. "Yes, I know," he said, with some understanding, "you just never had the gift—if you want to call it that—to be the celebrity type."

George Brent was an essential ingredient of *The Fighting 69th,* and a solid actor and fine gentleman George was and is. After a very productive career in the business, he was able to satisfy a life's dream and return to his native Ireland for the retirement years. There is always something very comforting in knowing that an old friend has obtained his heart's desire, and I felt very happy for George. Not a long while ago as I was in the doctor's office getting my yearly physical in came an Irish-American I know, a horseman. He had been in Ireland not long before and I asked him how George was doing over there. "Oh, he's back," the man said. "Living down around Rancho Santa Fe."

So I scurried around to find out where George was, got him on the phone, and said, "George, I'm pleased to hear you're here. But what happened?" He said, "It's still a wonderful country, but, oh, Jim—those Irish mornings! You freeze. So the wife and I decided that the only place to be was where it was sunshine most of the time."

Part of the stock company was also called out to do duty in an item called *Torrid Zone,* a zone Warner's created on its back lot in Burbank. This is the picture I call *Hildy Johnson Among the Bananas* because it's really just a reworking of the Hecht-

MacArthur play *The Front Page*. Because the story line of *Torrid Zone* was so terribly predictable, I thought that just to effect *some* kind of change, I'd grow a mustache. It was really rather a silly-looking thing, but at least it was inoffensive. Inoffensive, that is, to everyone except the top brass. They gave the producer of the picture, Mark Hellinger, some emphatic hell about my little peccadillo. Mark, a happy-go-lucky guy with a flair for high living, came to me about it.

"Jim," he said, "the boys in the front office want to know why you grew the mustache."

"What's the matter with it?" I said.

"The brass claims it takes away some of your toughness."

"They know all about *that,* don't they, Mark? Hell, what do we want to do? Sell the public the same piece of yard-goods all the time? Let's have some variety."

Mark went back to the front office and conveyed my feelings. With that, the powers-that-be said, "Oh, the hell with it. It's just Cagney being his own difficult self again." In any case, *Torrid Zone* proved to be a money-maker—and I suspect that the fact had precious little to do with my mustache one way or the other.

In those days when pictures had to be cranked out on an undeviating schedule, one went everywhere for screen stories, and sometimes the original sources were good, sometimes bad. *City for Conquest,* which we did in 1941, is an example of the former, being taken from Aben Kandel's novel of that name, a novel with some fine things in it. I went to work on that picture with something of a will for just that reason. I played a truck driver turned fighter, and so I dieted and trained myself from 180 pounds down to 145 in order to do the fights. To get in the ring and be convincing one has to be in shape or one drops down dead.

I did all my own fight scenes; the prospect of a few punches in the puss never bothered me. I was hurt once in the picture. They threw in a fair-to-middling fighter who had been a pro, and this was his first appearance in pictures. I think he figured one job was going to make him a star because when the director said, "All right, action!" the fighter got a little excited. He threw one, hitting me right on the chin. A dandy. I swung around so the camera couldn't see me, and I laughed as I said "Oh, you son-of-a-bitch." I got a kick out of it because his face was absolutely stricken when he realized what he had done. Then I threw one, hitting him square on the chin, and his knees buckled. We mixed it up and finally the director said to cut and to print it.

"My God, Joey," I said, "did I hurt you?"

He said, "I saw my whole family. I saw my whole family. I saw my Uncle Ben, my Aunt Minnie, I saw my Cousin Davey. I saw them all."

From that point we got along fine. That night I went to see my mother in the hospital where she was confined with multiple strokes, which left her bereft of speech. But she could certainly see, and as I walked into her room, she looked up and said, "Ooooohhh!" I asked her what was the matter, and she indicated my cut eye and lip. I said it was nothing and that the boy hit me accidentally. But Mom made a sound indicating she thought he meant to hurt me; then I explained the whole thing, telling her how the fighter saw his whole family after my blow. Then she thought it was funny, as indeed it was.

I worked like a dog on *City for Conquest*. There were some excellent passages in Kandel's novel, passages with genuinely poetic flavor, and all of us doing the picture realized that retaining them (as we were doing) would give *City for Conquest* distinction. Then I saw the final cut of the picture, and this was quite a surprise. The studio had edited out the best scenes in the picture, excellent stuff, leaving only the novel's skeleton. What remained was a trite melodrama. When I realized what they had done, I said to hell with it, and that cured me of seeing my pictures thenceforth. I even wrote a letter of apology to the author. Yet *City for Conquest* did well at the box office, which ought to prove something or other.

Also successful at the box office but sticking much more closely to the original author's intention was *Strawberry Blonde*, taken from James Hagan's Broadway play *One Sunday Afternoon*. It was turn-of-the-century nostalgia, very tastefully done, and we were shooting it under its Broadway title. But my mother came to visit me while we were shooting. It was part of our family legend that when she was about sixteen she went to a dance with a fella named Eddie Casey. That happened to be the very night the song "Casey Would Waltz with the Strawberry Blonde" was first introduced. Because Mom was a strawberry blonde, she and Casey were inevitably the feature of the evening. So, as a tribute to my mother, we renamed the picture.

The day we shot the scene where I waltzed with my strawberry blonde, Rita Hayworth, my mother came. There it all was— 1890, just as she remembered it: waiters with handlebar mustaches and colored vests, and the foaming beer steins. There were even pretzels on the table. She made only one comment, and an authoritative one, too. "Jim," she said, "pretzels didn't come in until later!"

Even with a script as good as that, one is always looking for the little touches to add. My character, Biff Grimes, a dentist unjustly sent to prison, has to work on the warden's teeth. I had the property man hang up a striped coat in the hall outside the warden's office. As I appear in the shot I am all in stripes, too, and I bustle into the hall, remove my striped coat, hang it up, and don the striped coat already hanging there. It is, of course, an exact duplicate of the coat I've just taken off. Don't you know I had a letter some time later from a sailor aboard a battleship in Alaskan waters saying that this very funny bit absolutely made his day. His letter certainly made *my* day.

My mother's presence in California reunited our entire family at least temporarily. Brother Bill, of course, had been in California since 1931, and by 1941 he was an associate producer at Warner Brothers. Ed came out with Mom in 1938, and not long after retired from medicine. He was later to be very valuable as a script adviser when brother Bill and I founded our own little motion picture company. Harry came out to join us all in 1941, continuing with his medical practice.

There were always family get-togethers, of course, and parties with close friends, but the big Hollywood bash where one wanders around large groups of people making the talk has always seemed to me a complete waste of good living time. This is not to say my Bill and I haven't gone to the large parties and occasionally enjoyed ourselves, but for the most part we chose not to. In fact, on occasion my wife and I have *given* so-called big parties, but we always had people in who were real fun, like George Burns and Gracie, Dick Powell and June, and of course the Frank McHughs, the Hacketts, the Pat O'Briens.

At one particularly memorable party we had the people I've just named and several others—Bob Montgomery and Betty, George Murphy and Julie, and Esther Williams with her then husband, Ben Gage, who had a good baritone voice. After dinner with all the fixings, I went into the big living room and I said to the piano player, "When I kick the rug over to the piano, you segue directly into 'Swanee River,' and by the time I get to the piano, George Burns will be right behind me." And as I did that, getting to the piano and kicking the rug, I turned and there was George Burns. We went right into a soft-shoe break, George did a step, then I did a step, and that was the start of the evening's fun.

Dick Powell had a wonderful way of singing "When Irish Eyes Are Smiling" off-key. It was one of the funniest things I've ever heard. In order to sing off-key deliberately, one must have excellent pitch, and Dick used to kill me with this crazy thing. Wherever we were, if there was a piano available, I'd always ask Dick to do "When Irish Eyes Are Smiling." It never failed.

That night Ben Gage sang, Frank McHugh told his stories as only he can tell them, O'Brien was on, and Andy Devine did his bit. Everybody *there* did something, making it one of the most pleasurable evenings I've ever experienced. One of the guests, a lovely gal, said, "This thing has to be repeated," so she invited everybody at the party to come to her house a week or two later. "I'll send you each a note," she said, which she did. In the note she added, "Black tie." Well, the same cast appeared—everybody ready, willing, and able, but whatever the psychology of it was, the black tie killed the whole fun of the evening. Nobody got on, nobody made a move. A real shame. Those things are hard to repeat.

In the early 1940s my Bill and I received additional impetus to remain basically home folk. Our children—Jim, Jr., and Cathleen ("Casey," we call her)—came along, and what we did before we adopted them I just don't know. When Jim came along in 1941 we were really overwhelmed by the experience, and the fact that he was a perfectly beautiful little guy didn't hurt any either. Shortly after Jim came Casey, also beautiful, equally important to us right from the beginning. I recall the wonderful, wonderful feeling of having them both sit on my lap as I told them stories. I told all the great traditionals, Little Red Riding Hood, the Three Bears and Goldilocks, but I made a great mélange of them. To this day Jim and Casey talk about those stories. For example, I dreamed up an account of the three and a *half* bears. In this version the three bears had a cousin who came to visit them, but he was a half bear only because he had length and width, no thickness. In fact when this bear cousin turned sideways, you couldn't see him. Now, this little cousin bear was walking through the woods one day when he saw Goldilocks being followed by the big, bad wolf. The wolf obviously being up to no good, the little bear challenged him. The wolf went on the attack, but the smart little bear outfoxed him—to mix animal images a bit—by turning sideways. Naturally the wolf couldn't see his prey and he was very upset. And so on. This was a typical incident in those fairy tales I told my kids and they, I'm glad to say, are now telling the same stories to their kids.

One day when our kids were young my Bill heard Casey talking to little Patty, the daughter of the Kuniyukis, the Japanese couple we had asked to help us out in household chores during the war. Little Casey and Patty were discussing something about sex they'd obviously picked up piecemeal at school. So my Bill gently got Casey to one side and explained that what the girls were saying was untrue. She told Casey that any questions she had on the subject would be answered frankly and clearly. Casey asked my wife if she would tell her *anything;* my Bill said yes, anything. "All right, Mom," Casey said, "how do you make cardboard?"

One day I was walking down to the barn with young Jim, and in a perfectly clear and beautiful soprano he began singing the "Marseillaise," in French. He didn't realize I was paying any attention. Later, I started to sing "*Allons—*" and I stopped to ask him the next word. He didn't know what I meant. I explained that I had just heard him sing the song in French. He said he didn't have any idea, and he didn't. Never sang it again, couldn't get him to sing it. Now figure that one out if you can.

When Casey was little, we didn't even know she'd taken the trouble to learn The Lord's Prayer. But my Bill heard her one night as she knelt beside her bed, "Our Father, who art in heaven. *Hollywood* be thy name. . . ."

Another vital part of my family was making her presence felt in the world. Allow me to do a little justifiable bragging about my sister Jeanne, a very bright gal who decided she was going to be an actress after she graduated from Hunter College at nineteen. When I went to her graduation exercises, she announced her plans to me, speculating that I might be surprised to hear them. Indeed I was, because Jeannie was an expert linguist, speaking a fine French and German. On top of this, she had a very well-rounded personality. I had an idea she might become a teacher.

"Darling," I told her as she stood there in her cap and gown, "you are a lot smarter than I'll ever be, and I'm not the one to have any opinions about what you should do with your life. And if acting is what you want to do, you go ahead and you just do it. Though there's one thing you have to do, my pet. You have to get into a gymnasium."

Jeannie had been the total student type, had never put one foot in front of the other athletically, and I knew that among other things, development of stamina was essential for her future in what is physically a very demanding business. She agreed, and I said, "Get into a gymnasium, or better still, get to work with Johnny Boyle and have him teach you to dance for a solid six months. If you do that, moving from one place to another will never be a problem for you." She said fine. That was June, and she started the dancing regimen in California with Johnny at once. I was in the East until November, and on my return what I saw absolutely stunned me. Jeannie was doing wings, cramp rolls, all kinds of buck dancing—really intricate steps, with full assurance and control. By the time *Yankee Doodle Dandy* came along, there was no doubt she could play that lovely dancing lady, Josie Cohan, beautifully. It was, if I may say so, type casting.

We Cagneys have a deeply engrained sense of privacy. I wasn't particularly aware of it at the time, but we would never intrude upon each other. Each family member would do what he or she had to do without bothering the other. Jeannie, of course, chose her own row to hoe when she decided to go into show business. An interesting thing to me was that after she got working in the theatre she would be doing jobs here and jobs there and I never knew about them. As I was on the West Coast and she was on the East Coast, I found out only later that she had done many plays and many TV shows that I had never known anything about. I think the basic thing in her thinking was that she didn't want to trade on her brother's name and get him involved in her career. She never wanted to become a burden, and she certainly never has been.

In 1941, I did *The Bride Came C.O.D.* with Bette Davis. I have never seen that one so I have no firsthand information as to how it came out. But I have no reason to doubt Bette's word when her autobiography said, ". . . Jimmy, with whom I'd always wanted to work in something fine, spent most of his time in the picture removing cactus quills from my behind. This was supposedly hilarious. We romped about the desert and I kept falling into cactus. We both reached bottom with this one."

I think probably the only funny line in the picture came when hefty Gene Pallette ran across the desert in search of his daughter, followed by sheriffs and a group of frantic people. After huffing and puffing along, Gene suddenly stops dead still in the midst of all this fuss and furor and says, "What am I running for? I've got four million dollars."

Certainly of more moment was the next one, *Captains of the Clouds,* my first adventure in Technicolor. It was a pretty detailed look at Canada's role in the British Commonwealth Air Training Plan. Shot on location with the Royal Canadian Air Force, this was quite a piece of work at times, and I mean work.

One day we had just finished a scene—Alan Hale, Dennis Morgan, and I—in which we had to bring in a plane, jump out of the cockpit onto the tarmac, then sprint fifty or sixty feet to get out of camera range. And this we did *all* day. The first take, the plane wasn't where it should have been; the second take, *we* were where we shouldn't have been, and so on down the line. Nothing right, just one miss after another. We wore out three sets of cadets, and all they had to do was walk between us and the camera as the plane taxied in. When we left the set at day's end, the three of us were bone tired.

We went to the hotel, showered, and sat around in the room talking and trying to relax. There was a knock, and I opened the door to find a young man who asked if Alan was there. Thinking he knew Alan, I invited him in, and Alan and Denny assumed that the fella knew *me.* As it turned out, nobody knew who the hell he was. But he made himself at home immediately, grinning from ear to ear, at his ease. Finally this genial character turned to Denny and me and said, "Now tell me. Is there any work to it at all, or is it all play?"

Here we were, hardly a leg under us from this day of jumping in and out of planes onto the tarmac, weary all the way through—and we get a query like this. I looked at the fellas, they looked at me. Then Alan Hale, who was a big, pleasant, wonderful guy, looked at the stranger, and said to him, "Get out of here, you stupid son-of-a-bitch!," and threw him out.

The one consolation for all the hard work we did was the kind of person you worked with. Alan Hale, that wonderful guy we all loved. Always in a good humor. Dennis Morgan, also a nice, nice guy. George Brent and I pulled a pleasant gag on Dennis once. This was at the time when Denny had just joined Warner's, and George, who wasn't in our picture, had come to visit me on the set. Denny, of course, is a big, good-looking Scandinavian (his real name is Stanley Morner), and on this occasion he was standing before the camera for a lighting session; all lights were on, and he was unable to see us standing beyond the camera. So George and I started this rib by speaking very seriously, letting our voices carry in to Denny. "Good-looking guy, isn't he?" George said.

"One of the best around here," I answered. "And you know something else?"

"What?"

"He sings, too!" I said, "and now can you imagine a guy with his physical equipment and *also* a singer? Can you think of what he'll do to these gals around here?"

"My God," George said, "what now? How do we cope with this?"

Denny couldn't take it any longer, so he peered out from behind the camera, just barely able to make us out. Then he saw me grinning and he said, "Oh, you bastards!" So we had a good laugh and I brought George over to meet him. Wonderful people.

As the years wear on, I look back at those people and think about them. When they were around, I really enjoyed them, but now I realize that I *could* have enjoyed them more. But the picture business has always been such a hysterical one and the demands on attention so great that one didn't have time to really savor everything to the fullest—particularly your friends. That is one of my regrets.

6

Psychologically I needed no preparation for *Yankee Doodle Dandy*, or professionally either. I didn't have to pretend to be a song-and-dance man. I was one.

In just about every interview, in most conversations, one question emerges unfailingly: what is my favorite picture? Many people assume that one of those knock-down-drag-'em-outs would be my choice. A discerning critic like Peter Bogdanovich can't understand why I choose *Yankee Doodle Dandy* over *White Heat* and *The Public Enemy*. The answer is simple, and it derives from George M. Cohan's comment about himself: once a song-and-dance man, always a song-and-dance man. In that brief statement, you have my life story; those few words tell as much about me professionally as there is to tell.

Yankee Doodle Dandy began, of course, with Cohan's interest in seeing his life story filmed. He was aware that this was a valuable property, and he wanted it done with style and taste. As I got the story, he went first to Samuel Goldwyn, then committed to a picture with Freddie Astaire. Goldwyn submitted the idea to Freddie, who didn't think it was for him. Cohan took it to Paramount, but after listening to their offer, he turned it down.

At the same time that arrangements were being made for Cohan to sell his life story, my brother Bill was hard at it looking for a story with genuine American flavor. This was uppermost in his mind when he came upon the Cohan possibility. Bill then put everything behind getting the story done with thoroughness and depth. Bill wanted to do the Cohan story as a 100 per cent American experience principally to remove the taint that apparently still attached itself to my reputation—a reputation now scarred by my so-called radical activities in the thirties when I was a strong Roosevelt liberal. Anyone of that background was usually colored pinko in hue at the very least. Bill chose *Yankee Doodle Dandy* with deliberation.

Meanwhile, my friend Ed McNamara had been in a show with Cohan. Cohan sounded him out about me, and Mac was able to point out that I had been a song-and-dance man for years in vaudeville. On learning this, Cohan's people took the idea to Warner Brothers with the proviso that I do it, all of this taking place without my knowledge. Then the Warner's script for the picture—written by a man named Buckner and approved by studio head Hal Wallis—was sent to me at the Vineyard for approval. I read it with incredulity. There wasn't a single laugh in it, not the suggestion of a snicker. And this was a script purporting to be about a great American light entertainer, a professional humorist, a man who wrote forty-four Broadway shows, only two of which were not comedies. I said to brother Bill, "It's no good, I won't touch it. But I tell you what I'll do. I'll give it a blanket O.K. now if you put the Epstein boys on it to liven it up and inject humor."

Julius and Phil Epstein were two very bright lads. They had invigorated the scripts of *Strawberry Blonde* and *The Bride Came C.O.D.*, and I knew and liked them both. The minute Phil and Julie went to work, I made the deal to do *Yankee Doodle Dandy*. When I got to California to prepare for shooting, I wanted to be as close to Cohan as I could, so I had Warner's hire Johnny Boyle. Johnny had been featured on Broadway in *The Cohan Revue of 1916*, had actually staged dances for Cohan, and knew Cohan's personal dancing style firsthand. From Johnny I learned Cohan's stiff-legged technique and his run up the side of the proscenium arch. Johnny and I had a great time rehearsing together, but it was hard, hard work—so hard that Johnny hurt one foot badly enough to be virtually incapacitated for dancing the rest of his life.

Despite that, we got the rehearsal job done—almost. In the dancing business, you must have the steps so set in memory that you don't have to think about them. You must go over them unendingly until they become completely automatic. The very first number in *Yankee Doodle Dandy* for me was "I Was Born in Virginia." I got a few rehearsal licks in with Walter Huston, sister Jeannie, and Rosemary de Camp—the other three Cohans—but I went on to the shooting stage not knowing entirely what I was going to do. It got by, but I didn't feel right about it. Then we came to the "Yankee Doodle Dandy" number from *Little Johnny Jones*. Again not enough rehearsal and again apparently nobody noticed it, but I did. There was a rigidity in certain areas of the number because I wasn't always sure of what the next step was going to be.

As time wore on, we got the so-called dramatic scenes behind us, and the comedy scenes. It all added up finally to some good work, and I was reasonably happy with it. But by the time we scheduled the "Off the Record" number from *I'd Rather Be Right,* I was so dog-tired that at one step in the routine which I knew well—one of my old steps I'd been doing for years—I went blank. I just couldn't think of the step. I said we'd do it again, we went, and I blanked again. Finally I told Mike Curtiz, the director, that I was so damned tired that I couldn't think of my own step, and that we'd better call it a day. He explained that we would have to finish the shot that day. I asked him how long he wanted to be on the set. "Mike," I said, "I can't think of the next step when I get there. I'm tired."

Mike called the front office, and Jack Warner swore I was holding up the scene because I wanted the extras to get another day's work. This was as far from the truth as it was possible to reach. Had I been able to get through the day with that number behind me, I would have been exhilarated. But I daresay Jack Warner thought I was just being difficult. I wasn't, but my poor brain was.

In the non-musical parts of the picture, with the Epstein boys at work, the dialogue was nice, easy stuff. Moreover, I had the pleasure of working with that superlative actor, Walter Huston. I knew we were working well together when after we finished Walter's death scene in which I collapse weeping in his arms, I turned to hard-boiled Mike Curtiz and saw tears streaming down his cheeks. "Cheeses Chrisdt, Jimmy," he said, "beautiful, beautiful." That may have been the ultimate compliment.

Naturally, brother Bill and I were concerned about what George M. himself would think of the picture. During the making of *Yankee Doodle Dandy,* Mr. Cohan was confined to his Fifth Avenue apartment bearing up bravely under the cancer that was to kill him later that year, 1942. He had a representative out in California, however. This was Ed Raftrey, 300 pounds of amiable Irishman who was nevertheless under strict orders to pounce on anything he knew Cohan wouldn't like. Inevitably in a story that is, as we made quite clear in a prefatory title, only *based* on a person's life, certain liberties with the facts had to be taken. Brother Bill in showing the final cut to Ed Raftrey was very apprehensive. Bulky Ed sat at one end of a long lounge for the viewing, and my 220-pound brother sat at the other. During the showing, nothing came from Raftrey. Not a sound, not a move. Then as the story came to a close, the lounge started to shake violently. Big Ed was sobbing, thereby relieving brother Bill vastly. Fortunately before George M. died, he was able to see *Yankee Doodle Dandy*, and he gave it his blessing. I like to think that this only contact we had was professionally appropriate: one song-and-dance man saluting another, the greatest of our calling.

So *Yankee Doodle Dandy* turned out to be something I could take real pride in. Its story abounds in all the elements necessary for a good piece of entertainment. It has solid laughs, deep warmth, great music. And how much more meaningful are those patriotic songs today in view of all our current national troubles! *Yankee Doodle Dandy* has lots of reasons to be my favorite picture. When I got the Academy Award that year, I was able to say my few acceptance words with some feeling: "I've always maintained that in this business you are only as good as the other fellow thinks you are. It's nice to know that you people thought I did a good job. And don't forget that it was a good part, too. Thank you very much." Praise from your peers generates a special kind of warmth.

And my peers were very much on my mind in 1942. In September of that year, I had become president of the Screen Actors Guild, and we all had a deep professional worry to attend to. Gangsters were muscling into pictures, and they decided that the Screen Actors Guild offered lucrative opportunity for exploitation. Whereupon the Chicago Mob sent out to California one George Brown, head of the projectionists' union. Mr. Brown was rather colorful; he always had a mouthful of chewing tobacco, with brown spittle running down the side of his mouth, all that in great contrast to a spotlight-sized diamond ring he always wore.

He brought a couple of hoods with him, and together they tried to take over all the labor unions in Hollywood.

Fortunately, the government stepped in, and they found that Brown and a man named Bioff had shaken the motion picture producers down for about a hundred thousand dollars. The Screen Actors Guild pressed the case against these extortionists, and Brown and Bioff were convicted. They went to prison, and so did Joe Schenck, who did a year at Danbury. It was not an easy time, and there were moments when things were a bit tender. My Bill got a phone call one night, and a man assured her I'd just been killed in an auto accident. She didn't panic but called the Guild office where I was at a meeting. There were other planned surprises. The Mob had arranged for a several-hundred-pound klieg light to be dropped on me while on the set, but George Raft heard about it, told the Mob that I was a friend of his, and the project was canceled.

Another group occupying my attention in 1942 was the Actors' Committee of the National Victory Committee. As chairman of that unit I can attest we did a lot of night work. I remember Porter Hall saying that our epitaph should read, "Committeed to death." But it was little enough we were doing for the war effort, and as was only fitting, a number of us were called together to go out on the road to plug the sale of war bonds. This was the Victory Caravan, which went cross-country for three weeks. We had quite a group. There were Cary Grant, Pat O'Brien, Frank McHugh, Laurel and Hardy, Bert Lahr, Groucho Marx, Charles Boyer, and others, plus the most beautiful assembly of gals anybody ever cast an eye upon. Among them were Claudette Colbert, Joan Bennett, Joan Blondell, Arlene Whelan, Olivia de Havilland—such beauties. Bob Hope was our emcee until Chicago, where Bing Crosby took over.

I had never worked with Bing before, and here was a great opportunity to see at first-hand the way this great performer did it. Bing had always been a remarkable fella to me, and I had always thought that everything he did was so relaxed and effortless. Not so. At our opening show at Soldier Field, Chicago, there was a

20. The original Four Cohans: Jerry, Nellie, Josie, and George.

21. Their able impersonators in *Yankee Doodle Dandy:* Walter Huston, Rosemary De Camp, Jeanne Cagney, and James Cagney.

22. *Man of a Thousand Faces* (1937) shows the most gentle one.

23. As the plant-happy captain. *Mister Roberts*, 1955.

24. With producer and pal, Bob Montgomery, and two marines. *The Gallant Hours*, 1960.

25. As Admiral "Bull" Halsey. *The Gallant Hours.*

crowd of 130,000, with 30,000 of them behind the platform we were working. Bob Hope was doing his stuff and he said, "Well, I know you're waiting to hear the Groaner—," and the place went crazy. Bing walked out to a reception for which the adjective "triumphant" is inadequate.

He stood there in that very humble, charming way of his, wearing a brass-buttoned blue coat, rust trousers, brown-and-white shoes, and a light green shirt that seemed to verify the legend that he's color blind. After the audience explosion died down, Bing said, "Whadda yez wanna hear?" and they exploded again until the stadium walls nearly buckled. After they subsided, he said, "Ya wanna leave it to me?" and they blew up again. Finally, he said, "Hit me, Al," and our orchestra conductor, Al Newman, started his boys off on "Blues in the Night." They had played only the first two bars when the audience went into rapturous applause once more. Bing finished that song, and never in my life have I heard anything like it. I got the traditional goose pimples just standing there, listening. He did another, same thing.

And if ever I wanted a demonstration of how it felt to live through that old vaudeville phrase, "What an act to follow!," this was it. I was next on the bill, waiting in the wings to do my little stint, "Yankee Doodle Dandy." Fortunately I had some good natural support in the form of my Civil War soldier's uniform, eight cute girls, plus eight American flags blowing in the wind. I danced my brains out, the girls waved the flags energetically, and the entire cast came out and joined in "The Star-Spangled Banner," and this was, I can tell you, an experience.

But I've almost forgotten the point of this story, which is that when Bing came offstage, the perspiration on him was an absolute revelation to me. Here he had been to all appearances perfectly loose and relaxed, but not at all. He was giving everything he had in every note he sang, and the apparent effortlessness was a part of his very hard work. I can remember the first time I had any fixed opinions about Bing. Up at the Vineyard in 1938 I heard one of his radio shows, and I knew at once that this was a most extraordinary fella. I actually started to write a piece about him,

"The Miracle Known as Crosby," but after a page or two, I stopped. I realized he was just beginning, and would add up to even more than he was. So I dropped it, thinking perhaps I'd save up my thoughts for the proper time. If this is the time, I'm glad at least to report my feelings about a man I always watch when he's available to public view.

There was much fun on the Victory Caravan, but typically I went to bed at an appropriate hour. Our two stay-ups were Pat O'Brien and Al Newman. They'd be up all hours of the night, talking and drinking, drinking and talking. After about three days of this, Pat, who always manages to look fresh, went into the barber shop early one day to have his usual shave. "Where's Newman?" the barber said. "Oh," said Pat, "I drank him at four o'clock this morning."

After *Yankee Doodle Dandy,* it became time to reassess my relationship with Warner Brothers. In the usual pattern of things, I'd leave them when the salary got inadequate, a truce would be suggested, and I'd go back at a salary increase, always with their explicit promise that if my box-office value went up, they would give me a new contract. Year after year it became a predictable bore; there was just no desire on their part to keep the promise. Each time I'd say to them, "Well, how about it, boys? Isn't it that time again?," and the inevitable reply was, "Business is very bad. We can't afford to make that kind of commitment now." Finally we made a contract where *I* had the option, and in this new deal I was supposed to be getting a percentage of the gate. I found they were doing some pretty fancy things with the books, so that marked the end of that. I walked out again, and brother Bill and I formed a little company to make our own pictures.

The major studios had a curious and very elemental point of view about their actors: anybody they paid a dollar to belonged to them, but body and soul. Quite simply, the studio owned you. It said so right in the contract if you looked at the fine print long enough. The loopholes were damned few and pinhole small.

So the Cagneys went on their own. Our first picture was *Johnny Come Lately,* a charming period piece about an itinerant

newspaperman in the nineties. Grace George, the gracious star of
many Broadway productions and the wife of the great Broadway
showman William A. Brady, was in the cast. But I think our
biggest accomplishment in *Johnny Come Lately* was to establish
as one of the hallmarks of Cagney Productions the liberal use of
good supporting actors. As *Time* magazine said about this, "Bit
players who have tried creditably for years to walk in shoes that
pinched them show themselves in this picture as the very competent actors they always were. There has seldom been as good a
cinematic gallery of U.S. small-town types."

Any number of times in pictures like *Johnny Come Lately*,
I've seen actors in secondary roles do their work so damned well
that I've walked over, put my arm around him or her, and said,
"You were great, goddamn it, you were great!" And they were
great, very often better than the actors they were supporting.

In 1943, because *Yankee Doodle Dandy* was still around, I
was asked if I would do a patriotic benefit at the Polo Grounds. I
agreed, and that afternoon was a thrill for me quite beyond anything before or since, because I had the opportunity to walk
among the heroes of my youth. What words can I find to say how
it was as I sat in the dugout talking to Babe Ruth, Walter Johnson, and Roger Bresnahan? Roger Bresnahan, one of the greatest
catchers in the game, was catching Christy Mathewson one
glorious time when my dad took me to a Giants' game. It was
Roger Bresnahan who influenced me to become a catcher, with
his superb style. And on this afternoon of the benefit, there I actually was shaking his hand and the hands of all those great stars
who were playing an old-timers' benefit game.

It had to be called an all-star roster: Ruth, Johnson, Bresnahan, George Sisler, Eddie Collins, Heinie Zimmerman, Irish Meu-
sel, Zack Wheat, and Red Jack Murray. Every one of them I had
worshiped as a kid. Everybody in the stands that day was hoping,
hoping, that the Babe would hit one out of the ball park, and
don't you know, he did. I wonder where in the hell one can find a
thrill to equal that these days? It may be hard for young people to
get such a kick now because I sense in America these years—and

I'm saddened to say it—I sense a systematic attempt to tear down our heroes. Eddie Robinson just said in his posthumously published autobiography about Charles A. Lindbergh, "To hell with his politics. He is our last, great hero." If ever our country needed heroes, it is in these melancholy days, and when I hear of things like the broadcast not long ago that said Thomas Jefferson slept with his slave girls, I am depressed. Maybe Jefferson did, maybe he didn't; in any case, why drag that in? What does that have to do with the greatness of this man? I've seen announcement of a projected story on George Washington purporting to prove he was drunk when he instigated a massacre of some French troops. This robbing us of our heroes is the heritage of some fine so-called liberal thinking that tries to kill one of the finest things we possess—warrantable pride in our past and the things that made us. Worship of the past? Nonsense. We can't escape our past. It's always with us, and we need the best that's in it.

This tearing down of our heroes has extended itself these days even to our national humor. The rip-down, pull-down, kick-'em-all-around type of humor has taken on undue influence and strength, I believe. I'm not the kind to dwell unduly on the good old days, but one of the many good things about the old days was the integrity of American humor. Kid national life? Sure it did. But never with a bitter iconoclasm that destroys rather than builds up—never destructively, scorning the general scheme of living in America. Ripping people apart, no matter how cleverly done, brings no smile to my lips.

During World War II, most of the entertainment world set about making personal appearances to sell bonds and entertain in camp or outpost those young men who had no chance to get to town. The air watches, particularly, were at their secluded posts for long days at a time. One Christmas night Ralph Bellamy, Frank McHugh, and I were having the holiday dinner at the Bellamys'. We got a telephone call that some kids on duty atop one of the Santa Monica mountains weren't going to get time off on that important day. We didn't even bother to finish dinner. We drove up to the lookout post, did the stale jokes, and I gave out a couple of songs. One began to realize that however little it was one had to offer in way of entertainment, how much it meant to those youngsters and how fully it was appreciated.

The USO was sending people all over the world then, and when they called asking if I would go to England, I said, "Why not?" When we crossed the Atlantic in 1944 on a transport ship carrying over thirteen thousand men it was, of course, vital for us to wear life jackets everywhere on board. The Nazi submarines were a formidable menace at the time. Each morning we had a drill so we could get to the lifeboats efficiently in case of a torpedo. One of the ship's officers, a man with a resounding Scotch burr, told us assembled one day, "Now, I want to tell you boys something. Listen carefully. There isn't enough life-saving gear on board to take care of everybody, but we've done the best we can. Not everybody will survive a sub attack. But I just want to give you this word of counsel: you *must* all remain in your assigned positions, because if you decide to go to one side of the ship or the other, you could capsize the whole business. So please be aware of that, gentlemen. I thank you."

One day during the crossing, some hours after our regular morning boat drill, the alarm sounded. The real thing. When I reached my assigned place, I found a tall young stranger, obviously lost. He was ashen and so, I suspect, was I. He looked down at me and said, "Well, hello." I returned the greeting, and he, certain that this was his last day of life, said, "Nice to have met you, Mr. Cagney. Today's my birthday." But he celebrated it without worry. We had a false alarm, although the wolf pack was all about us.

The concentration of troops aboard was incredible. They were even sleeping on the decks. And some of those lads were massively seasick. One officer came to me and said his company's top sergeant, a really great guy, was so afflicted with *mal de mer* that he wanted to die, and would I come down and say hello to him? I went down to D Deck, and here was this tall, bright, tough sergeant stretched out in agony, looking like a pile of old clothes.

"Hello, fella," I said.

"Oh, hello, Mr. Cagney," he said painfully. "Glad to see you. I just want to say that I have never felt so bad in all my life. Never—in my entire life. I want to tell you something—and I mean it. When I get to England—*if* we get to England—if *I* get to England—I'm going to marry me an English girl or a Scotch girl or whatever they've got over there. I don't care. Because I am going to stay over there for good. I ain't never gonna ride on this ocean no more."

All during our voyage one thought remained uppermost in my mind: would I see my kids again? Every morning I'd awaken in my bunk with the sensation of their arms around my neck. But we made it. The old *Mauretania* arrived at battered but unbeaten Liverpool in January 1944. There were sunken ships all around the harbor. As I got off the ship and walked across the dock, I looked up at the *Mauretania* and saw the thousands of boys up on the decks, waving. I thought of what one well-placed torpedo could have done to those fine young men. I went on tour at once, and I recall especially a paratrooper camp in Wales. I began the performance, part of which was to give a dancing lesson. I did a complete routine to show the fundamentals, and at the finish I was, of course, breathing hard. A little soldier yelled, "Hey, Jim, you're gettin' old." I agreed, and then to give us all a little fun, I asked him to come up on stage with me. He was a typical, friendly little Brooklyn roughneck. I said, "Now, I'll tell you what I'll do. I'm going to have the piano player begin, and I'll start dancing. All you've got to do is hop from one foot to another *eight* times on each foot, in time with the music."

He agreed, and away we went. I was doing a simple time step, but what he failed to realize was that he was doing an exercise totally new to him. Before I got through the first chorus, he was ready to collapse, thus earning him a rousing chorus of razzberries from his pals. After it was over, he stopped, gasping for air.

"This is for you, Jim," he said, handing me a piece of fused lead and copper.

"Thanks very much. Where'd you get it?"

"Where'd I get it? It hit me in the goddamned head!"

The medics had removed this piece of shrapnel from his skull, and he was saving it. But he gave it to me, and I've kept it proudly at home all these years.

Dancing, if done consistently and as part of a measured regimen, is a form of health insurance. One of the reasons I feel good now in my mid-seventies is that I have learned one must never surprise the heart. I estimate that exercise enough to get you out of breath twice a day helps you stay fit. Also for my exercise I have had fun with judo, principally under the tutelage of Ken Kuniyuki, who had been a top judo instructor in Los Angeles prior to Pearl Harbor. After that he was packed off with many other Japanese-Americans to the detainment center at Pocatello, Idaho. When he got out of there there were damned few jobs for Japanese, and my wife and I were delighted when Ken, his wife, and their little girl agreed to come into our household. In addition to his regular work, or perhaps as *part* of his regular work, Ken, a fifth-degree black belt in judo, taught me some essentials. I had a *dojo* built, which is a kind of ring with a heavy pad on it, and we would work out there. During one of those sessions Ken gave me a massive heave-ho, and I went over his head, landing on mine. I heard a loud crunch in my neck, and I lay there, stunned, as Ken asked me if I was all right. I asked him to try my neck, and thankfully it was all right. I was lucky to have landed sideways; a few inches more the other way, and I would have been in permanent trouble. Judo was fun, but its permanent legacy to me was an undue physical buildup. It put an eighteen and a half neck on me, and from the waist up, I got heavier.

Knowing judo was a professional need for our 1945 Cagney production, *Blood on the Sun,* in which I played an American reporter of the 1920s who uncovers the incipient plottings of the Japanese imperialists. My costar in *Blood on the Sun* was Sylvia

Sidney, who played an Eurasian girl, and convincingly, too. One day Sylvia was making a costume test before the camera, and I watched her as she turned around, and then around again, looking as elegant as any Shinto princess and twice as lovely. Now, Sylvia is Jewish, and I with my affection for Yiddish can't resist the opportunity to use it when I can. This was a very piquant occasion because she looked to be a thousand leagues away from her actual ancestry. To tease her, from behind the camera I said, *"Zee gigt aus vi a Chinkeh!"* (She looks like a Chinese lady!). Imperturbably, and without stopping her pirouette before the camera, she said, *"Fa vus nit?"* (Why not?). It is some accomplishment to be talented, beautiful, *and* funny.

I think my mother merited those adjectives. Her talent was for living bountifully in poverty or in plenty, her beauty was of both the external and internal variety, and her sense of humor was indestructible. When my expanding fortunes allowed me to buy the Martha's Vineyard farm, I hastened to share my deep love of the country with Mom. Not long after my purchase, there appeared on the market a nearby summer home, very spacious, just right for a large family with a gracious big porch all around it, and with a view of the water you couldn't match anywhere. I bought it with the specific purpose of letting it be the summer place for Mom, Harry and Ed with their kids, for Jeannie—for everybody. My mother came up, and for all I knew was enjoying herself fully. But one morning she said, "Son, let's have a talk."

"What is it, Mom?"

"I know you want the best for all of us."

"That's right."

"And you got this place because you love it, and it *is* beautiful. It's everything you'd want in a country place. But, son, my idea of the place to be is on the corner of Forty-second Street and Broadway, in a big plate-glass window, sitting in a rocking chair, watching it all go by."

She had spent about ten days in the country, and that for her was a little more than enough. She went back to the city and never came back to the country again. I had assumed that because I loved the country with vehemence that she would share my passion. So, again, she was teaching me one of life's fundamentals: deep enthusiasms are never automatically transferable.

When she came out to live in California it was in a Hollywood apartment near the city's heart. We had her to enjoy for only a comparatively brief time because in 1945 a number of strokes came in tandem, and with two doctor sons in attendance, we learned quickly that all symptoms were discouraging and irreversible. Ed was living in her apartment, taking care of her, and Harry lived just a few blocks away. I got a call from Ed, and I went down. "We'd better get Jeannie and have her come home," he said. Jeannie was then in a New York show, but she came quickly.

The greatest piece of pantomime I have ever seen in my life was not performed on any stage or in any film. It was done by my mother on her deathbed. Because the strokes had deprived her of speech, she had only her eyes and one fully functioning hand to use. The four boys were in the room when Jeannie arrived. She came in and embraced Mom. Then we all got around and hugged Mom warmly, and she made a vocal sound that was unintelligible but spoke volumes of love for us.

It happened that two brothers were on each side of Jeannie. Mom then raised her functioning arm, the right. She indicated Harry with the index finger of her useless hand, she indicated me with her second finger, she indicated Eddie with her third finger, and with her fourth finger indicated Bill. Then she took the thumb, moved it to the middle of her palm, and clasped the thumb tightly under the other four fingers. Then she patted this fist with her good hand and made a single wordless sound. We understood at once that Jeannie was the thumb and we four boys were to take care of our girl. It was a movement totally simple, totally eloquent, totally beautiful.

Mom died about two months later. She was sixty-seven—and there was hardly a day of those years that had not been spent in giving.

7

So much blarney has been written about Hollywood's Irish Mafia that a few words on the subject would seem salutary. There was a period in the early 1940s when Pat O'Brien, Frank McHugh, Ralph Bellamy, Spencer Tracy, Lynne Overman, Frank Morgan, and I would get together once a week, have dinner, and make the talk. That's all there was to it. Simply go into the week's happenings, and if there was a story to be told, or jokes to be let loose, that was the place and that was the time. Laughter and fun among some old friends, nothing more. But Hollywood being what it is—that flatulent cave of the winds, John Barrymore called it—all kinds of ridiculous connotations were put on our little get-togethers.

Sidney Skolsky, always a man to make news where he could, first called us the Irish Mafia. That there was some Irish blood can't be doubted, but Bellamy has not one drop of Irish blood, Frank Morgan was German, and Lynne Overman is also a Teutonic name. I am one-quarter Norwegian. But "Irish Mafia" had a titillating ring to it, and so it remained in public print until, inevitably, time rang in its changes. First Lynne died, then Frank Morgan. Bellamy left to do Broadway plays, and Frank McHugh also moved East. O'Brien and I were the only two mainstays remaining, and because he was on the road so much, we could only see each other occasionally.

Of all that group of intriguing fellas, Spence Tracy might conceivably have been the most intriguing, possibly because he was the most disturbing. It is, I think, a truism that phlegmatic people don't last in the acting business, and two excellent non-phlegmatics were Bette Davis and Spencer Tracy. Many years ago in answer to a question from Robert Garland of the New York *World-Telegram* as to who I considered the most outstanding of the up-and-coming people in Hollywood, I said Bette Davis and

Spencer Tracy. Up to that time I had only seen Bette once, playing a secondary part in a 1932 picture, *The Rich Are Always with
Us,* and Spence I only knew from a second-rate thing called *The
Murder Man.* They were both so remarkably alive that when they
walked into a picture they carried it all with them. They were
both incipient thyroid cases. Early in life Spence did have a
serious thyroid problem, and anyone with thyroid trouble *is* in
trouble. Spence's problem was a slightly unsettled personality. He
was a most amusing guy, a good companion who told great stories
beautifully—but there was always the tension that was tangible.
You can *feel* the stress in such people.

I told Robert Garland that without any doubt the American
public was going to hear from Spence. Not only did the public
hear from him for years after, but once we became friends, I sure
as hell did. My phone rang more than once at three or four in the
morning, and that unmistakable voice would start talking without
any preamble whatever. Never a "Hello" or a "Hi!" or even a
"Good morning." Just—"What are you doing, Cagney?"

"Sleeping. It's three in the morning!" Spence would ignore
me completely and go right on with whatever was on his mind.
The horrible part of all this was that invariably what he said was
so interesting that I'd snap wide awake, and stay awake.

One time I was at the Vineyard, the phone rang, and again
without a "Hello" or "How are you?" was that intriguing voice.
"You're going with me, aren't you?"

"Going where, Spence?"

"The funeral."

"Whose funeral?"

"Frank Morgan's funeral."

"Frank? Frank died in California. He was buried out there."

"No, no. I'm in New York. They're going to have the funeral
here. The body was shipped to New York. The whole family and
all the friends are supposed to be there. You and I are expected."

I explained that I couldn't make it, much as I wanted to. I
was caught in an appointment with some hydraulic engineers

from Boston who were coming to put a ram in up at the farm, and getting away was an impossibility.

"Oh, don't. Cagney, don't do this to me."

"I just can't get away. But keep me posted on what happens, will you?"

He promised, and two days later the phone rang. And again without a preliminary, that voice. "Oh, oh, oh!" I asked him what the matter was.

"Oh—you should have been there."

"Why?"

"Oh, I went to the cemetery with Ralph [Frank Morgan's brother]. I took one look at Ralph and I said to someone, 'There's no point in bringing *him* back. Just leave him.'"

"Spence, don't you know that Ralph is ten years older than Frank?"

"What's that?"

"Ralph is ten years older than Frank."

"No kidding. You mean that Ralph is sixty-nine years old?"

"Yes."

"Oh, what the hell! Then he looks great!"

In 1946, I played Joe, the champagne-tippling philosopher in William Saroyan's *The Time of Your Life*. Cagney Productions bought this beautiful Pulitzer-Prize play because of its great human warmth, and we gave it what James Agee described admiringly as "a loving production." That would be right.

When brother Bill and I first thought of buying the play for pictures, it was decided that a personal contact with the author was mandatory. It was my job, representing our little company, to tell Bill Saroyan what we planned to do. This was very simple. We were going to shoot the script as he wrote it. No nonsense of adaptation, which is frequently an ominous word used to cover up the alteration of something superior into a vehicle for a screen "personality." We were concerned with the total personality of the charming play itself and no more.

I met Bill Saroyan by appointment at The Players, but getting that appointment was almost like a Saroyan play and the sometimes bewildering simplicity that characterizes them. I called him at his home in Oyster Bay, and a girl answered.

"Is Mr. Saroyan there?" I asked.

"Who's calling?"

"Jim Cagney."

"Who?"

"Jim Cagney."

"Just a minute." Many minutes went by. The girl came back.

"*Who* is this?"

"Jim Cagney."

"What do you want to see him about?"

"We bought a play of his, a thing called *The Time of Your Life,* and we're going to do it. And I suppose I have a date with him to tell him what we propose to do with his play, and talk it over."

"Oh, just a minute." The girl left, and another long wait intervened. The next voice I heard was a man's.

"Hello."

"Mr. Saroyan?"

"Yeah."

"You and I are supposed to have a get-together."

"Uh huh."

"When do you want to do it?"

"I don't know."

"Why don't you come in to The Players, and we'll have dinner there and talk it over."

"Where's this?"

"The Players."

"What's that?"

"A club—on East Twentieth Street. Can you come in tomorrow?" And more of the same. I'm just stating the preliminary of the conversation. But come in he did, and Bill Saroyan is quite an interesting piece of work. At the time he had jet-black hair in high pompadour, a complexion white as bleached parchment, and strong, dark, protruding eyes. He came down to the bar, where I was waiting. I walked up and introduced myself. Like Spencer

Tracy, he didn't say hello, just stood there, listening. "Listen to that," he said. I couldn't hear anything but the typical sound of The Players' bar: the billiard balls clicking, a radio faint in the background, the slapping of cards on the bridge table, the bartender shaking a cocktail. Bill was hearing these sounds, too, but they meant something to him. "It's kind of a symphony, isn't it?" he said. I said I thought you could call it that, and we sat down.

He sat down, looking pleasantly wild-eyed. We did the small-talk thing, and then, sauntering over to our table came a fellow Player, Allan Reagan. Allan was known to take a drop or two. For years Allan and I had been swapping old obscure songs with each other, and this day he stood before our table, drew himself up to his full six foot two, pointed his finger at Saroyan, and sang very loudly and solemnly:

> If you don't like your Uncle Sammy,
> Then go back to your home o'er the sea
> To the land from where you came
> Whatever be its name;
> But don't be ungrateful to me—
> I said, to me—
> And if you don't like the stars in Old Glory,
> And have no use for the Red, White, and Blue
> Then don't act like the cur in the story,
> And bite the—"My Country 'tis of thee!"—
> And bite the hand that's feeding you!

It would seem almost impossible for Saroyan to get paler than he was, but he did. I said, "Mr. Saroyan, this is Allan Reagan." Allan greeted Bill genially by first name and sat down for some more small talk. After Allan left, I asked Bill what disturbed him so much. "I thought he was accusing me of being un-American," he said. It's fascinating that Saroyan, a man who wrote so many good comedies, apparently confines his sense of humor to his writings.

Cagney Productions lost half a million dollars on *The Time of Your Life*. The cameraman and the director had two weeks of rehearsal without turning a crank. They wanted to block it all out and plot exactly where they were going, shot for shot. This was laudable enough. Then when we finally got going, they decided they were going to do something else. Thus we lost two very expensive weeks of shooting time. The lack of decision on both their parts was, let me say, unhelpful.

Notwithstanding the terrific money loss, the picture was beautifully done. We received a lovely letter of thanks from Bill Saroyan saying, among other things, that when he watched the film he forgot that he had written the play. "I was too busy enjoying it," he said, "to care who wrote it."

We had fun making *The Time of Your Life*. My brother Ed, with wit ever ready, brightened one of my days during shooting by appearing when we were doing a scene in which champagne was served. We used real champagne—Mumm's—and when shooting was done for the day, I asked Ed if he'd like a little glass. Ed was a teetotaler, but he agreed for conviviality's sake, so I poured him a half glass. Next morning I asked him how he was.

"Not so good, Jim."

"Why?"

"Hangover."

I was incredulous. "You mean from that little bit of champagne?"

"Oh, no," he said. "Not just that champagne. I mean a hangover from mixing my drinks."

"God, what did you do—go home and start belting down other stuff?"

"Oh, no," Ed said. "Don't you remember in 1939 when I came out on the Grace Line with Mom and we got off for a little visit in Havana? Just to celebrate, I had a half glass of beer."

In the cast of *The Time of Your Life* we were lucky to get that great ex-vaudevillian, James Barton, who played Kit Carson, the charming old pathological liar. Jim's own career sounded as if it was fiction, but the engrossing thing about it was that it was true in every particular. He was the consummate performer. A great dancer, he could sing songs that would lift you out of your seat, and he could do a dramatic scene with the best. My brothers and I often tried to get Barton to put his fantastic life story between covers. He started on a showboat, and not the glamorous side- or sternwheeler, but an unpowered old schooner that sailed from town to town down the Chesapeake. The actors would warp the boat into a pier and then bring it around so that the stern sheets would be facing the dock. After taking chairs out of the hold and putting them on the dock, they'd do a come-on show to get the townspeople in, and follow up with the regular show in the stern sheets.

When Jim was a boy in the nineties, black-face comedians were extremely popular, and he became one at the age of seven. He started to dance at that age, too, learning terribly intricate Irish jigs and reels, which I couldn't begin to do even after he showed me. Jim did everything in show business, all the hokeypokey shows, burlesque, vaudeville, Broadway musicals, then the legitimate theatre and films. He did it all.

When the Actors Equity Association called the famous actors' strike in 1919 that stopped all the shows on Broadway, there was a benefit performance for the Actors' Fund. Some of the striking actors had contracts with various producers that specified that if they appeared on any stage they would be in violation of contract. What some of them like Ed Wynn did was to go to the benefit performance and, pointedly ignoring the stage, do their acts right in the aisles, thus technically honoring their contracts. Caruso, Al Jolson—all the great show business names were there, but it was the unknown Jim Barton who closed the show, and kept closing it that night. The audience wouldn't let him go. Nobody knew this little burlesque comedian, but that night he topped the top ones, and in *Variety*'s phrase, had to beg off. After he and his encores were exhausted, he just looked at that audience he had won so solidly and said, "Thanks for the use of the hall!," and exited. "Thanks for the use of the hall" is now a saying with some currency in show business. Jim and I talked about that line, and he told me where he got it.

"There was a saloon in Chicago," Jim said, "near where I

was playing at State and Lake. I was in the saloon having a beer when a man came in. He was a derelict, a real bum, but his vocabulary and diction were impeccable, a flawless speaker. It was the old face-on-the-barroom-floor routine come to life. He began to quote Shakespeare, and everyone was so taken with him that they began to buy him drinks. They kept buying him drinks. Finally he had lapped up so much sauce he became objectionable and they had to throw him out. Right on the street. The drunk picked himself up, staggered back through the swinging doors, and intoned in his sonorous voice to them all, 'Thanks for the use of the hall!'" Jim appropriated the line and used it when and where applicable.

After our pleasant encounter with Saroyan, I went back to Warner Brothers to do *White Heat*, and although ultimately it turned out to be a good picture in a number of ways, it was another cheapjack job. There was a limited shooting time, and the studio put everybody in it they could get for six bits. A case in point. There was one character in the script who looked as if he could lighten the proceedings—the fat boy, Tommy. Who else better to lighten proceedings and bring a much-needed spark than Frank McHugh? I asked for him, and Warner's yessed me and yessed me until the first day of shooting, when they told me they just couldn't get Frank. I found later Frank had never been asked.

The original script of *White Heat* was very formula. The old knock-down-drag-'em-out again, without a touch of imagination or originality. The leading character, Cody Jarrett, was just another murderous thug. For some kind of variant, I said to the writers, "Let's fashion this after Ma Barker and her boys, and make Cody a psychotic to account for his actions." The writers did this, and it was a natural prelude to the great last scene in the picture where I commit suicide by pumping bullets into the blazing gas tank I'm standing on.

But what an opportunity was missed with a number of things simply because time and money weren't placed second to quality! Casting the role Frank McHugh should have played with a straight actor was typical of this. In one scene the character gets a letter from his sweetheart, but it was so thoroughly marked over by the prison censor that it couldn't be read at all. As it now appears, that scene is dimensionless; with Frank doing it, it would have been rich. Nothing against the young fella who played the part. But I'm sure he wouldn't mind my saying that his experience stacked up against Frank's was strictly no contest. Here was an all-too-typical example of the studio trying to save a bit of money and thereby failing to achieve a potent bit of added flavor that would have helped the picture.

To get in the Ma Barker flavor with some pungency, I thought we would try something, take a little gamble. Cody Jarrett is psychotically tied to his mother's apron strings, and I wondered if we dare have him sit in her lap once for comfort. I said to the director, Raoul Walsh, "Let's see if we can get away with this." He said, "Let's try it." We did it, and it worked.

Not long ago a reporter asked me if I didn't have to "psych" myself up for the scene in *White Heat* where I go berserk on learning of my mother's death. My answer to the question is that you don't psych yourself up for these things, you do them. I can imagine what some of the old-timers would have said in answer to that question. They would have laughed aloud at the idea of an actor pumping himself up with emotional motivations to do a scene. The pro is supposed to know what to do, then go ahead and do it. In this particular scene, I knew what deranged people sounded like because once as a youngster I had visited Ward's Island where a pal's uncle was in the hospital for the insane. My God, what an education that was! The shrieks, the screams of those people under restraint! I remembered those cries, saw that they fitted, and I called on my memory to do as required. No need to psych up.

This psyching-up process, which I consider so wasteful and intrusive on the actor's job, reminds me of the time I was working with a certain young actor, quite a competent young man it seemed to me. I said to him, "Let's run the words," so we went into my dressing room and did just that. A good rehearsal, and he was just fine. Next day after shooting the scene the director said we'd have to do it over. I asked why and got a vague reply, so we did it again, and this time I went to see the shot in the viewing room. There I realized what the difficulty was. This young man was breaking the first rule of acting: he was doing it for *himself*, not the audience. He was psyching himself up to *be* the character, instead of just understanding the character and playing it for the audience.

This self-involved kind of acting reminds me of a story Ralph Bellamy tells. Ralph was on a TV set one day, shooting, and a young man in the scene was saying to the director, "What is my motive here? What am I thinking of?," and all that junk. The director finally blew up and said, "Never mind what you're thinking of, never mind what your motive is. Just do as I tell you. You're holding up production." Afterward, a little second cameraman said to Ralph, "These guys make me think of a man who is in a rather unique position. He's standing on the corner of Forty-second Street and Broadway in a pouring, drenching rain, on a cold, cold March morning at 3:00 A.M. And he's peeing down his leg, feeling so warm and comfortable—and nobody else knows what's going on!" Which, in my view, just about sums it up. These privately oriented actors, like the young man I did the scene with, aren't telling the really important people—the audience—what is going on.

I have a delightful footnote to the *White Heat* experience. At the time a marvelous review of the film by John McCarten appeared in *The New Yorker*. Mr. McCarten expressed regret that in years just prior to *White Heat* I used to terrify moviegoers, but unfortunately as time went by I seemed to have mellowed. He pointed out how wrong he thought that was, and congratulated me on returning to the ratfold. He went on: "Despite all the scatterbrained nonsense of the script, Mr. Cagney, representing a homicidal maniac whose favorite girl is his dear old two-gun mother, comes up with a performance so full of menace that I hereby recommend him for whatever Oscar is given an artist for rising above the asininity of his producers. . . . [The police] not

only are bold, brave, strong and willing but use more para-
phernalia in capturing enemies of society than were required for
the invasion of Normandy."

I wrote Mr. McCarten an appreciative letter. Four or five
years later, Bob Montgomery and I were being inducted into the
Salmagundi Club as honorary members, and as we sat at our
table a man came to us, stood there smiling, and said hello. It was
Mr. McCarten, who announced that he had come over to ask me a
favor. "Name it," I said. He wanted an inscribed picture of me to
be given a friend of his. I made a note of it and asked for the
name to inscribe. "Kitty Paradise," Mr. McCarten said. I asked
him if he was kidding, but he assured me that this was the lady's
name. In due time I sent the picture to him for forwarding, and
thought no more about it. But ten years later it was oddly comforting for me to read in *Art News* that Kitty Paradise had been
made head of the kitchen department of the Salmagundi Club.

~ 8 ~

A couple of questions frequently asked are: 1. Do I ever watch
my old films on television?, and 2. If I do, what ones do I best
enjoy? The direct answer in both instances is, 1. Hardly ever, and
2. The ones with the music and dance. I can be puttering away
with something upstairs, and if one of my oldies appears on the
tube, my Bill never calls me down unless it's one of the musicals,
and even then I never come down to watch the so-called dramatic
bits, only the dance routines.

I can only repeat what I've repeated before: once a song-
and-dance man, always a song-and-dance man. There is something special about it. You have to like dancing very much to do it
because it is such hard work. The dance you've done you must
have liked very much or you wouldn't have done it. One also

recalls all the hard work that went into a thing that turns out well. There are certain moments in my musicals that I find uniquely attractive. I think of the finale of *Yankee Doodle Dandy* doing the wings as I went down the White House staircase from the President's office. That was a moment I particularly enjoyed and particularly like to view again. When we did *The West Point Story* in 1950, there was some pleasant dancing to be done. There was some critical hooting and hollering about the key plot line: the assignment of a Broadway musical director to actually live the life of a West Point cadet for some weeks. Such a thing just couldn't happen, some critics said. Only it did. Both Westbrook Pegler and George M. Cohan did just that at various times. In any case, in *The West Point Story* beautiful Virginia Mayo and I did a number that I thought was some of the best dancing we ever did. It's still a pleasure to look at because it showed some versatility and humor, things I prize highly and always strive for.

This very effective number, "Brooklyn," was staged by a little red-haired gal named Godfrey, who had been with Jack Cole. She put the entire involved sequence together in about ten days. I did my rehearsal dancing with her, and because she weighed about a hundred pounds, it was no effort at all. I tossed her around like a rag doll, doing all the things that were required with great ease. Then in came Virginia Mayo to take her place as my partner, and here was quite a difference. Very beautiful and talented Virginia is not exactly a wraith of a girl. It took a little adjustment but it worked out well, and Virginia in her usual fine style made that number something I always enjoy watching. In Chicago recently I had the solid pleasure of seeing Virginia again and sharing good reminiscences over lunch. She was starring there in *No No Nanette!*, as beautiful and talented as ever.

After *The West Point Story*, I was in excellent condition, as I always am after having trained down to fighting trim and dancing weight. One morning just after wakening, however, I stretched, and apparently with some violence, because I pulled a spinal disk out of place. This was a disk that had been ruptured when I landed on my head in the judo session with Ken Kuniyuki. That displaced disk produced a paralysis in my left arm to such a degree that I couldn't raise my hand above the waist. It was a very serious business, but I procrastinated by failing to go to the doctor for a few weeks. I finally got to New York to see Sid Gaynor, the orthopedic man for the New York Yankees, and he recommended an operation. However, my brothers Harry and Ed were dubious, and they told me that if I used some sense, the injury would repair itself. I took their advice and just took it easy. Now my arm is in excellent condition, and my hand is functioning properly. The only thing I do lack now is the dexterity that I used to have in playing Spanish guitar. I can no longer make the spread. But my hand does work, and I use it without any sign of disability.

I went back to playing a tough one when Cagney Productions did *Kiss Tomorrow Goodbye* from the novel of that name by Horace McCoy. We made this picture on a deal with Warner Brothers whereby they would give the banks (where we owed money for the loss involved in *The Time of Your Life*) the first five hundred thousand dollars the picture made. One of the attractions of *Kiss Tomorrow Goodbye* was that damned good actor, Luther Adler, who taught me an acting trick I have remembered. Luther's really chilling moment in the picture came as he was sitting at a desk, just about to look up at me. Instead of lifting his face and looking at me at the same time, he lifted his face only, his eyes remaining hooded, looking down. *Then,* after his head was fully raised, he lifted his eyelids and stared slowly at me with infinite menace. Such a little thing but such a powerful thing. I had never seen an actor do that in my life, and I have been around a bit. Later I suggested that particular bit of business to Dana Wynter to use in the Irish picture we did, *Shake Hands with the Devil.* And when she whipped those big brown eyes from the ground at me it was a decided jolt.

I had seen the exciting Maxwell Anderson and Laurence Stallings play *What Price Glory* on Broadway in 1924. With Louis Wolheim and William Boyd both raunchy and tough as Sergeant Quirt and Captain Flagg, this was a pretty zesty piece of work. It had been remade into a pretty good picture in 1926 with Victor McLaglen and Edmund Lowe. Despite all these favorable ante-cedents, *What Price Glory* had never struck me as being anything up my street *until* I heard it was going to be made as a musical. I warmed to that idea immediately and decided to take it on. Then when John Ford was brought in as the director, he vetoed the idea of a musical. "What's wrong with the original?" he asked. That's a question that can only be answered negatively, but I was recruited on the basis of its being a musical, and I wouldn't have done it otherwise. Still, I was committed at that point, and I did it, but not, in Shakespeare's phrase, "for my ease."

John Ford had a slightly sadistic sense of humor. It's hard to resist the impression he occasionally allowed things to occur in order to satisfy this inner enjoyment. One scene in *What Price Glory* required me to come out of a building, exhilarated by the thought of going on leave, jump into the sidecar of a motorcycle driven by my sergeant, and drive off. Before the scene, Ford, smoking that tiny pipe the Irish call a dudeen, came over and said, "Do you really want to ride with this guy?" I answered, "Why not?"

This guy was the actor playing the sergeant, Bill Demarest. Bill had actually driven motorcycles in combat during World War I and knew these machines down to their tiniest nut and bolt. I assured John that I saw no harm in riding with Bill.

"Why?" John asked, with drawn-out deliberation.

"The script says so."

"Well," he said, taking a draw on his pipe, "you don't always do what the script calls for, do you?"

"No, you know I don't. But this one seems reasonable."

"Well, all right. But *I* wouldn't." And with that he turned and walked away, still sucking on the dudeen.

When time came for the shot, I dived out of the building on cue into the sidecar, and Bill jumped aboard the motorcycle. Now, Bill was wearing hobnailed boots, and what neither of us realized at the time was that the rubber had worn off the motor-cycle's brake pedal. We began our ride down a steeply graded hill, and to the right just beyond the hill's curve was a stone wall. To the left of the curve was what we call a parallel, a stand on which lights for the scene are hung. On this occasion, a little electrician stood in front of the parallel with an arc trained on us for the proper illumination. Bill and I roared down the hill about forty miles an hour, and as we came down toward the curve, Bill's hobnailed boot slipped as he applied the brakes. Knowing that hitting the wall would be catastrophe, he turned left and we crashed into the parallel, hitting the electrician and breaking both his legs. The motorcycle's handlebar whipped around catching Bill in the groin, knocking him silly. Luckily, I had managed to brace myself as I put both arms in front of my face. I was stunned, but Bill and the electrician had to be taken to the hospital. Once they had been taken care of, I limped up the hill to find John Ford standing there, quietly sucking on his dudeen. As I drew abreast of him, he looked meditatively at me and said, "What'd I tell ya?"

Some time after *What Price Glory,* I did *Run for Cover,* a Western that seemed to promise something deeper in content than the average Western. This is a picture I *did* see because an old friend wanted to look at it and I went along for company. However, it didn't move me in the viewing to anything very much but anger. We had tried to make as offbeat a Western as possible, but whoever cut the film was evidently revolted by anything but clichés. As a consequence, little things that the director, Nick Ray (a good man), and the actors put in to give the story extra dimension were excised very proficiently. The result was just another programmer.

In 1954 John Ford called me and said, in effect, how about a nice vacation? He had *Mister Roberts* in the planning stages and wanted me to play the captain. There were several distinct attractions held out: just a few weeks' work in Honolulu and, most pleasingly, the role of Doc was to be played by Spence Tracy. It all looked like fun. Spence, however, had no intention of playing Doc, I discovered later, but John was lucky enough to get Bill Powell for the part, a hell of a guy, a hell of an actor.

Things worked out quite well. Bill Powell and I didn't work very much, swimming and sunning on the beach, telling stories and relaxing in depth. Then we'd get the wigwag from the ship we were shooting on to pop over to work, so we'd go out there, holler, jump up and down, then back to the beach again. Most pleasant.

I met a young fella on that picture, a nice young fella. I had actually seen him on television some time before, and I was much struck by him because he knew how to be funny without being brash, a thing rare among young comedians. One sees a great deal of brashness these days masquerading as comedy, but it's a repulsive mask. When I saw this young man on television he went all through that hour show without missing a beat. An apple-pie performance. I missed the credits on the program, so I didn't know who he was. I called the office of Cagney Productions and said, "Sign this young man if we can get him, whoever he is." We weren't able to, but three weeks later I saw him again on TV, this time playing a straight dramatic role, that of a drunken reporter. I called brother Bill and asked him to track the young fella down, but in the interim John Ford had seen the young man.

The young man, Jack Lemmon, to my pleasant surprise had been cast in *Mister Roberts*. I had preceded the company to Honolulu, so when they all came in, I met the plane.

I said to Jack at this, our first meeting, "Hello, son. How are you?"

"How do you do, Mr. Cagney?"

"Just how left-handed are you?"

"What?" He was startled.

"Just how left-handed are you?" I repeated.

"I don't know what you mean."

And he didn't. I then explained that in the first television show I saw him do, an adaptation of the old play, *The Man from Blankney's*, in which he played a soda jerk, everything he did—wiping the counter, sweeping up, moving objects—was done with his left hand. I refreshed his memory. "Oh," he said, "I'm not left-handed at all."

"Not at *all?*"

"As a matter of fact, I am so *right*-handed that I decided I was going to play everything left-handed and make it a mark of the performance. For the challenge of the thing." To me this was proof that a mind worked in back of Jack Lemmon's acting, and that he was determined to bring some distinction to any part he was playing.

The shooting began, and *Mister Roberts* progressed in good order. Then I realized that upcoming was a scene with Jack, as Ensign Pulver, that I had found so funny in the reading that I realized it would be marvelously so in the playing. The difficulty was that it was *so* funny I had serious doubts about my ability to play it with a straight face. I talked it over with Jack. I said, "We've got some work ahead of us. You and I'll have to get together and rehearse that scene again and again and again until I don't think it's funny any more." He agreed because he had the same feeling about the scene. So we got together and did it and did it and did it. But every time I came to the payoff line in the scene, "Fourteen months, sir," I just couldn't keep a straight face. Finally, with enough rehearsal we thought we had it licked. We came to filming time.

The scene has Pulver down on deck where he suddenly sees me and scampers up the superstructure to get away. I see him and say, "Young man. Young man!"

"Yes, sir."

"Come here." He does, and I look at him with great curiosity. "Are you one of my officers?"

"Yes, sir."

"What's your name?"

"Pulver, sir."

"What do you do?"

"I'm in charge of laundry and entertainment."

"Oh." Pause. "How long have you been aboard?"

"Fourteen months, sir."

Now—I submit that this is one hell of a funny little scene: the commanding officer of a naval vessel finally meeting an ensign who had been ducking him during their voyage for well over a year. I used to collapse every time Jack said "Fourteen months, sir," but when we filmed it, I was able to hang on just *barely*. What you see in the film is the top of Mount Everest for us after our rigorous rehearsals. It still kills me every time I think about it. *Mister Roberts* is the kind of thing I enjoy doing best in the non-musical field, drama with comic overtones. Comedies as such have never appealed to me particularly. I have always thought a story with opportunities to drop in some fun was a lot better than trying to be funny for two solid hours.

While on location for *Mister Roberts,* I was sent the script of *Love Me or Leave Me,* the Ruth Etting biography. I took one read-through and said, "My God, yes. We go with this one." There was nothing to be added, nothing to be taken away. It was in fact that extremely rare thing, the perfect script. I was so pleased to find one that didn't need any help, any devices. Among other things, I was pleased with the biographical honesty. The protagonists in this powerful account of Ruth Etting's life were all alive: Ruth, Martin "The Gimp" Snyder, the first husband, and Johnny Alderman, her second husband. Under the usual "life is just a bowl of cherries" Hollywood reworking, their taut and bitter story would have emerged as a romp through the primroses. Fortunately the participants were well paid for their authorization, and the facts could be faced uncompromisingly. All of this, too, was set against some pretty good music.

"Gimp" Snyder was a belligerent man who had suffered a prenatal polio attack that gave him a decided limp. After seeing the picture, he said to someone, "Where did Cagney learn to imitate my walk?" I didn't. I had observed people with that kind of affliction, and very early in planning the role, I knew that doing the limp with any kind of support gadget would be intrusive. So what I did was very simple. I just slapped my foot down as I turned it out while walking. That's all. Mr. Snyder liked the picture from all accounts. I learned later that the part had been offered to Spence Tracy and he turned it down, why I don't know. It was a damned good part.

I had worked with Doris Day before, of course, in *The West Point Story*. But I really didn't get to know her then, and there certainly was nothing substantial for her to do in that picture. But when we started on *Love Me or Leave Me*, I saw something in her I hadn't noticed before, or maybe it was just coming into bloom. I don't know. She had matured into a really exceptional actress, and I told her so. I said, "You know, girl, you have a quality that I've seen but twice before. There was a gal named Pauline Lord who created the title role in Eugene O'Neill's *Anna Christie*, and I'm also thinking of Laurette Taylor. Both these ladies could really get on there and do it with everything. They could take you apart playing a scene. Now, you're the third one."

In thinking about Doris, Pauline Lord, and Laurette Taylor, and the single quality they shared, I am also put in mind of the Barrymores—Ethel, Jack, and Lionel. They had that quality, too—and if I had to put that quality into a word, it would be "unshrewdness." It is that part of a personality that immediately evokes from the audience the response of, "Isn't that nice?" Walter Catlett had it, too: wide open as a barn door, no guile at all. *Un*shrewd. In all of these people there is a beautiful basic simplicity stemming from their lack of guile. And that lack of guile photographs.

I have always said that shrewdness unaccompanied by other balancing and compensating factors is a very unattractive quality. People who are just shrewd don't stay around long in the acting business. I've seen them come into show business and become shrewder and shrewder. They don't last. Acquisitiveness takes over. I know of one comedian who would never let anybody else have a laugh in his pictures. "That's mine, that's mine, that's mine." He was gone in three or four years. Sometimes, of course, that lack of guile can be tragic. At the end of his career, Jack Barrymore said to his manager, "Where did all the money go?" It was all gone. The same with his brother Lionel, and with Walter Catlett.

I'm sure Doris Day has a better business head on her than these people, but she shares with them the quality that makes people seeing such actors say instinctively, "Why, there's a person who wouldn't do *anything* to hurt me." This quality, coupled with genuine acting ability, is irresistible to an audience. I was explaining something like this to Doris between shots in the prison scene of *Love Me or Leave Me* when the director, Charles Vidor, came over. Charlie was an amusing and cynical Hungarian, and he asked us, "What are you talking about?"

"Just actor talk, Charlie," I said.

"What are you doing?"

"What do you mean, what am I doing?"

"I know what you're doing."

"All right, what am I doing?"

"You're telling Doris how good she is."

"That's exactly true—and I know you'll agree."

"I agree, I agree!" he said, laughing.

"Charlie, don't you like to tell people how good they are?"

"Yeah, sometimes. But only sometimes." Which was ever Charlie's way.

After *Love Me or Leave Me,* Doris went into the *Pillow Talk* things, and I for one have always considered that one hell of a waste.

I hardly thought it in the nature of things that I would ever be playing and, happily, dancing the role of George M. Cohan again, but thirteen years after *Yankee Doodle Dandy,* the opportunity presented itself. Bob Hope was putting *The Seven Little Foys* into work at Paramount, and the script called for the appearance of George M. at a Friars' Club banquet where he trades kidding insults with Eddie Foy. This segues into a challenge dance routine on a tabletop between Bob and myself. Bob's invitation to do George M. coincided neatly with my desire to lose fifteen pounds. So he and I rehearsed the dance for three weeks, and I lost my unwanted lard.

There was one bit of trouble. In the routine, I had included a step for my solo portion that I had been doing for years, but not for perhaps a decade before this. It's what dancers call a knee snap, basically a pick-up with a roll on each foot. This is a step that gives the knee quite a bit of extra work. After about a week's rehearsal with Bob, I found my knees had swollen, but I thought little of it. Came time to do the number with Bob on the table, part of which called for me to leap up on it, then turn and pull Bob up with me.

The cameras started to roll. Not anticipating any difficulty, I leaped on the table, and as soon as my legs hit, up each of them shot a screaming pain. I didn't change expression but reached down and pulled Bob up. We proceeded to do the routine with both my legs paining almost beyond endurance. When I looked at the scene later, there was no sign of agony or even discomfort on my face. I would guess this shows what long training can do if the need is there.

Right after the number I called Bob into my dressing room and showed him my knees. He couldn't believe it. They were full of fluid, easily twice their normal size. But in a few days they were normal again and I was all right. I guess at fifty-six even a long-time song-and-dance man can't expect to bounce around in quite the same way he did at, say, fifty.

꧁ 9 ꧂

Might I now digress—to the point? Digress, because for a time I move out of the chronological sequence of my days; to the point, because outside of my family, the prime concern of my life has been nature and its order, and how we have been savagely altering that order.

I don't think of myself in any active sense as a philosopher, but it is certainly true that I am given, and for long years *have* been given, to that part of the philosophical process called wonder. Wonder, I think, begins with simple curiosity and some form of marveling, leading inevitably to the asking of that vital question, "Why?," and all this in the hope that some solid answers might supply themselves. I find I am doing that increasingly in my life, and in taking my great concern for the land and assessing that concern, I ask many questions. Oftener than not, I find no answers other than this: many people are indescribably wanton in their despoliation of the land either through stupidity or a colossal selfishness—and I use "colossal" in its true or non-Hollywood sense.

I have, of course, been in love with the country from early childhood, and when the opportunity came to own some of it, I acted. I tried farming the Martha's Vineyard property, but its soil was not of the best, and getting help was difficult. Consequently, with the guidance of Bob Montgomery, who had a place near Millbrook in Dutchess County, New York, I found an ideal spot in that area.

In 1955, when I bought the New York farm, I grew even closer to the country, and now I think of myself in retirement years as essentially *of* the country. Not long ago I had the chance to see close up the entire span of the United States, and this heartwarming experience reaffirmed my pride in this great republic, but it also made me even more apprehensive about the encroachments on the beauty of the land, encroachments that don't in any way seem to be diminishing.

I set out to drive from Beverly Hills to my farm, and as I progressed along a multiplicity of roads and highways, a number of random thoughts came to me that I confided to a tape recorder, thoughts elemental to my interests. These brief thoughts I offer now are not, God knows, answers to great questions or problems, but perhaps in keeping with the spirit of wonder that has always been so active in me, they are questions and observations that are not only self-revelatory but concepts that I may need to ponder more and bring into sharper focus for myself.

Another essential reason for my using the tape recorder on that trip was to recall stories about myself that constitute much of this book's contents, and as I went from state to state along Highway 66, I was surprised at memories evoked at many turns. I had been an extensive traveler, albeit not a very luxurious one, in my vaudeville days, and this trip was partially a tour of reminiscence. But primarily it was a voyage of discovery. Always having been a lover of the New England scene, I have used that charming part of our world as a standard for beauty. For me there has never really been any place like it. But I must now make apologies to the various states we traversed; I hadn't realized how beautiful they are. But I am learning.

For instance, when I first moved to California, I sneered at the desert country and could see no reason why anybody should ever want to live there. Then, bit by bit, I gradually awakened to the unique beauties of the desert. On my recent auto trip, I came to realize similarly that each of the states we passed through has its own beauty. Oklahoma and Missouri, for example, seemed to possess a green unsurpassed anywhere, and I was much struck by the extent of their tree cover. My Bill was born in Iowa, and learning from her of that state's extensive wheat belt, I was expecting flat, uninteresting country. Wrong again! I was delighted to see the rich kind of beauty that surrounded my wife in her childhood. And instances like this could be multiplied right and left all along the winding paths of our trip.

But, of course, everywhere I went I saw the unrelenting oppression of man-made blight, and especially that blight under our very wheels. At various points on Route 66, I saw road widths that seemed unjustifiable, lanes added for no discernible reason at all. How does this happen? Years ago when the highway-building racket started, a lot of us conservationists, seeing the proliferating highways and interchanges, realized that this in time was going to be a formidable problem. These highway boys at last had found a racket that could be legitimized in the name of progress, interconnecting the country with needless concrete at one whopping fee per foot. It made me put a few words together:

Lay down the ribbon of concrete, boys,
And we'll divvy up lots of loot;
We do it all quiet and neat, boys,

At ten thousand dollars a foot.
We'll certainly take care of our friends, boys,
As we give the law the bend, boys. . . .

But why go on? This senseless destruction of the land has infuriated me for years. The wantonness of that land slaughter in California made me write a little note to myself:

Tear the tops off the mountains
And terrace the slopes,
For the land must be ready,
For dingbats and dopes.

If that sounds bitter, let me say I mean it to be bitter.

The tremendous physical change in our country, I suppose, has come slowly. But to me it seems abrupt. Driving with some friends from my farm to a Pennsylvania horse show six years ago, we had to go through New Jersey. It struck me tellingly. What, *what* has happened to beautiful New Jersey? Mile upon ugly mile, I saw nothing but gas stations, road signs, auto dumps, used-car lots, and strident billboards prevailing over the green land. And all this was six years ago. No telling what it looks like now, but I am making a fairly weighty guess that the green has diminished even more.

Driving from the West on my recent trip, I realized more than ever the tremendous job we have to do in reclaiming some of the land from the terrible onslaught of the bulldozer. With increased population, the bulldozer seems inevitable, but how saddening, how indefensible! A long time ago it struck me that progress takes its primary form these days in the pursuit of the buck. One must make his way in whatever way he can, of course, but it also occurs to me that what we are determines our life path. As I put it in another way:

What we are determines our basic needs,
And the needs decree each course of action.
No need, no action may be regarded as rule,
With self-satisfaction, however miniscule,

Calling the turn with utter finality,
Obscuring for all of us each stern, stark reality.
Seeing what we want to see, needing no other view,
Until crisis arrives in the form of catastrophe,
Functions then gone, will lost to atrophy,
Man's malignant stupidity collecting its due.

Not all highways feeding our cities are infestations. Driving into Tulsa, for instance, was a pleasant experience because it was clean and unmarred. Moreover, the city itself seemed to have no matchbox buildings, the characterless blocks set down helter-skelter in so many cities without any sense of form or proportion. I saw some tall buildings in Tulsa, but they seemed both functional and beautiful. A development we passed there was perfectly lovely, done in excellent taste, and attractively low-profile, in keeping with the Indian idea. So it can be done with foresight as the guideline.

Foresight is the necessary prelude to any harmony in human affairs. No one much remembers today the great figures in our country who foresaw so clearly the rape of our land as far back as eighty years ago. It's unpleasantly amusing to see pompous politicians on television speaking of their plans to preserve our ecology. To hear them speak, one would think they were the first to feel the needed concern. Nowhere do they credit the earlier figures in ecology like Bennett, Haupt, Carhart, Vogt, Osborne, Pinchot, and Teddy Roosevelt. These were the men who laid it all out for us to see, but we wouldn't look until it was perilously close to being too late. These great men are forgotten, and their warnings have been taken up by vote-hungry Tweedledums and, most recently, by the kids, who feel they've discovered ecology. Well, even the ones among them who only give lip service can be a positive influence if it makes their stupid elders realize what's going on.

It will take some awakening. Eighteen years ago the Conservation Foundation, of which I am a member, asked me if I would narrate a radio series telling the story of conservation, and I agreed, of course. The next I heard of it was an occasional com-

ment by a friend that I had been heard on these programs—at
6:00 A.M. Profit-hungry radio stations wouldn't dream of giving
these vital messages prime time when they would do a bit of
good.

For fifty years now I've been trying to do my own broadcast-
ing about ecology in my own way, never hesitating to let people
know exactly what I think about this hideous wasting of re-
sources. A friend of mine at a gathering one night brought up my
name and got this rejoinder from a man there: "Cagney! Oh,
that's the nut who goes around turning off the water in the
dentist's office." I proudly plead guilty. When I'm in the dentist's
chair and he has to leave for a bit, I promptly turn off that precious clean water until he returns. In these days of such drastic
clean-water shortage, it's folly to sit there and watch that good
pure stuff swirling away, unused. When people hear me tell this,
they laugh, and I tell them, "Mister, there's going to come a time
when you wish to God somebody had thought about these things
—because there is only so much water, and it's getting dirtier by
the minute."

A very good friend of mine for forty years on arising invariably turns on both bathroom faucets before he even starts to get
his shaving equipment together. I notice this every time I visit
him. It goes on for minutes, all that good water pouring down,
wasted. Frequently he will turn around and go back into the bedroom for something, and I will shut off the water while he's gone.
He comes back in, turns it on again, and doesn't even know it's
been shut off. Four decades this has been going on, and he's never
tumbled to the fact that I keep closing the faucets. Such a
thoughtless waste of gallons and gallons of that precious stuff, and
yet this is a thoughtful man in every other way.

As I drove across the United States recently it was borne in
on me again and again how beautiful so much of it still is—those
trim houses and yards of Pennsylvania farmers being typical of
the best in our countryside. Those industrious farmers—all I can
say is, bless them, bless them. And at one point just as I was lux-
uriating in their beautiful cultivation of land and homes, a grace-

less outdoor movie screen loomed up to scar the landscape brutally.

Ten years ago my Bill and I were driving through Spain, and along a highway leading from Barcelona I noticed a long row of enormous old eucalyptus trees, beautiful, noble trees, thirty to forty inches in diameter. As we drove along, feeling genuinely edified by their beauty, I gradually noticed that each of these trees had been ringed for death. The bark had been notched into the cambium, the layer where the food is drawn up from the roots to sustain the branches and leaves. This notching was the process whereby the trees would dry up, allowing them to be cut down more easily. On and on, mile after mile, those doomed trees stretched. They were being taken down, I discovered a bit later, because another highway was due for construction. "But why, why?" I asked. "On each side of that road there is a wide flat area where an added highway can be placed without disturbing the trees. Why don't they put it there?" The Spaniard I was talking to didn't know, wasn't concerned. What the hell, they were only trees. In a rage, I wrote:

> Man comes and the trees go,
> The waters soon follow apace.
> They make their way toward the mother sea
> In broad fingers of liquid lace;
> Carrying with them the willing land
> For which they have much affinity.
> Making up, as they do, with the good clean air,
> God's very own blessed trinity—
> Air, Soil, and Water.

Still distressed days later, I added:

> When one considers just what man is,
> Happy it be that short his span is.

If he were around longer, there'd be an even swifter journey from beauty to dry death, a journey that I, like Hamlet, would ache to think on.

As to ultimate responsibility for all this—and I don't believe this has occurred to anyone before—the *initial* move in the destruction of our environment unwittingly is ours, individually. There is the investment motive. These ruthless developers can only get their money from a bank. Banks function only to make a profit. They rent the money out. But—whose money are they lending? Not their own. They're lending *our* money, the public's money, and in this very tangible way the public is participating in the destruction of its own environment. When the chap at Martha's Vineyard bought acres and acres along the shore with the plan of putting up high-rise condominiums; when the man to the west of me at the Vineyard bought the acreage and started to put up houses cutting into the beautiful hills all around—and the beautiful stream, Roaring Brook, became as it now is, yellow and full of clay; and when the people to the east of me cut fifty-three lots out of the hills, and that soil was also washed down into Roaring Creek—all of these ravages were caused initially by money. We are all directly responsible in a very real sense.

The wasting of the world and the inner spirit of man that fights that despoilment I can only sum up this way:

> If God is the ideal quite unattainable
> And Nature's fierce logic is most unassailable;
> If we observe with great care the human condition
> As we hurry in haste down the road to perdition,
> One phrase is large on mankind's scroll:
> All is ephemera—except soil and soul.

⌒ 10 ⌒

Tribute to a Bad Man came in 1956 at a time when I was up on Martha's Vineyard. I had been working early in the summer, and I went up to take my ease there when Spence Tracy, then on location up a Colorado mountain, became ill. He couldn't go on with *Tribute to a Bad Man,* so Nick Schenck, the head of MGM, called and asked if I would jump in for him. There were some eighty people in Montrose, Colorado, waiting to get the job done. I was about as interested in working as I was in flying, which means a considerable level below zero, but after much gab, I agreed. I specified that I would need at least two or three weeks between jobs, and then I would come out and do it. Agreed, and I went out. The result was all right, I guess.

Also in 1956 I did one of my very few television appearances. I have only been on three or four times. There was a brief *Mister Roberts* scene on "The Ed Sullivan Show"; also on Bob Hope's show to introduce some beauty-contest winners; and a show for Bob Montgomery. The Bob Hope thing I did because an old friend, a makeup man, called to say that if I introduced a few young ladies, the makeup men's charity fund would get ten thousand dollars. With that spur, I did it, and a little song and dance with Bob. It worked out well enough, but I've had no real interest in television at any time. I simply couldn't work up any kind of enthusiasm for it.

My stint with Bob Montgomery was for his "Robert Montgomery Presents," a show called *Soldiers from the War Returning,* about an Army sergeant detailed to escort the body of a dead buddy home from Korea. I played it because I promised Bob that if ever I did any work on television, I'd do the first with him.

I get frequent questions about what kind of fella Bob Montgomery really is. I have tried very hard in these pages not to overuse superlatives about my fast friends, but this Montgomery man is just plain extraordinary. He is a chap raised with a silver spoon in his mouth who on ability and guts alone became the leader of the Screen Actors Guild, and in their first big fight with the Producers' Association, laid his career right on the line. Without hesitation.

He has more than proven his mettle over the years by tackling the big guns of the television networks. Single-handedly, too. But beyond the gutsy determination he evidences when a question of principle is at stake, he's a deeply read, wonderfully intelligent man with a great social flair. And he's humorous, God bless him, and when we're together, the laughs are incessant. He was, of course, a fine light comedian, doing all those things with Norma Shearer, Greer Garson, and those lovely ladies at MGM when it was *the* studio. But when Bob moved into the presidency of the Screen Actors Guild, he incurred great enmity, an enmity that still persists. He has been labeled by the high powers as "difficult" and "rebel." Or put it as it really is, when he feels something is right, he damned well stands up for it.

Example. He produced his "Robert Montgomery Presents" for many successful years, and in going to the 1956 season he told me the networks were trying to dump him, and if I did the soldier-returning-from-Korea production, it would get the Montgomery season off to a healthy start. Of course I was happy to oblige. I learned from Bob that the networks would not give air time to anything they didn't own part of, a part usually in the neighborhood of 51 per cent. This sharp little practice insured the networks' control of everything going out over the air.

Bob defied them. He went to bat by appearing before the Federal Communications Commission and by denouncing this kind of monopoly before Senate committees. Without any hesitation he said everything that needed to be said. Inevitably, perhaps, he was beating his head against a stone wall, because one man against a power structure that entrenched is the battle of the one against the many. He couldn't win. But that single stand of his had an ultimate payoff. In the past few years the FCC and the Senate have made the networks give up some of their monopolized time. Bob Montgomery started this ball rolling years ago.

A few months after the Montgomery television show, I addressed myself to a complex task. In doing the life story of such a great screen artist as Lon Chaney it belabors the obvious to say that I found it a challenge. The Chaney family was a fascinating one, and in preparing *Man of a Thousand Faces* for shooting we came across several stories about the Chaneys that for one reason or another we felt constrained from using. Now that the son, Lon

Chaney, Jr., has gone, it is possible to tell at least this fascinating and truly pathetic anecdote. Lon Chaney, Jr., was simply the professional name of that talented and very nice gentleman. His actual name was Creighton Chaney. It seems clear that his mother deserted the family, leaving Lon and Creighton alone. But the boy very doggedly persisted in trying to find his mother.

She had an unusual and distinctive name—Cleva. Creighton went to great lengths to find her and finally got a lead to her whereabouts. He made his way to a remote ranch somewhere out on the desert, full of anticipation that his long search was at last near its end. He knocked, and a woman came to the door.

"Yes?"

"Hello. My name is Creighton Chaney, and I'm looking for Mrs. Cleva Fletcher."

"What's the name?"

"Cleva—Cleva Fletcher."

"Oh, I'm sorry," she said. "No one here by that name."

Then, directed to the woman, came a voice from inside the house: "Who is it, Cleva?"

This infinitely sad story we were unable to use. The agonizing pathos of it—a desperately needed mother talking to a son she wanted no part of—that story seemed both crueler and larger than life itself.

One might think that my most striking memory of doing *Man of a Thousand Faces* would be the various makeups I assumed to duplicate Chaney's amazing skills, but actually the first thing I think of is Hank Mann. Hank, one of the original Keystone Cops and a key supporting player in the Charlie Chaplin troupe, had been in my first Hollywood effort, *Sinner's Holiday*. In meeting him again in 1957 during the Chaney picture, I was struck once more, as I always am, by the fact of total professionalism. Hank, and another authentic comedian from the golden age of comedy, Snub Pollard, did a scene in the picture as comic waiters.

Inevitably they did a pie-throwing scene, and anyone who thinks there is no art in the throwing of pies has not seen Hank and Snub at their finest moments. I learned much from them, one law of slapstick being that a real pie-tossing artist doesn't just stand there and take the pastry deadpan. I noticed, in a lesson I'll not forget, that Hank and Snub mugged royally when anticipating the pies coming their way, Hank, for instance, crossing his eyes and dropping his mouth. It was a great pleasure to watch those two consummate *farceurs* doing the thing they knew so well.

With some Hollywood years under my belt, I have obviously had quite a series of experiences with directors. Directors, like human beings, come in all sorts: very talented, talented, quasi-talented, untalented. It is a profession I have never envied. So when my old friend A. C. Lyles came to me in 1957 and asked me if I would direct his Paramount production of *Short Cut to Hell*, I was moved to do so out of friendship only. I said I would do it if he wanted me to, and he asked me how much I'd charge. "How about nothing? Is that too much?" I asked him. We shot this updated version of Graham Greene's *This Gun for Hire* in just twenty days, and that was long enough for me. Directing I find a bore; I have no interest in telling other people their business.

And doing just that is the heart of the director's job. Some directors tell you your business quite competently; others are unbelievably inept. As I've said, I have worked with really only two absolutely superb stage directors—George Kelly and John Cromwell—men who not only knew their business but the actor's as well. During most of my Hollywood time the directing business was not overcrowded with geniuses. My idea of a director was theatre-derived: one who could get in and show the actor all the specifics if needs be, all moves, all intonations. In other words, a *director,* one capable of directing you to do just what was required. With the exception of Billy Wellman, Raoul Walsh, Bill Keighley, and their kindred, there were few directors I met who knew what they were doing when they got in *front* of a camera to demonstrate. There was no reason why they should, of course. They probably never acted in their lives. But I always felt safer somehow with a director who knew at first hand what the actor's job was like.

One of my directors, Mike Curtiz, had been an actor in the Hungarian and German theatre. He arrived one day on the set with a very specific idea of how a particular scene should be played. I said, "Go ahead, Mike. Show me how you want it." He went in and played it with all the old fancy European techniques —brushing off the cuffs with a flick of the finger, reaching fussily for a cigarette and lighting it with a flourish, then putting his foot up on a bench, and proceeding to talk with one hand on the hip.

"All right, Mike," I said, "now I'm going to do just as you suggested. I want you to watch closely." I'm a fairly good mimic, so I got before the camera and did it exactly as Mike had worked it out. When I finished, I asked him what he thought.

"I guess I'm a pretty lousy actor, huh, Jimmy?" There was nothing further to say.

One time having heard that I was a bit difficult (something I admit to being when I strive to get a thing right), a director I know decided to put me in my place. After I finished the scene, I noticed he was looking at the ground. He had paid no attention to what we were doing in the shot. I said, "Let's go again," and we did. Same as before. He sat there, eyes on the ground. "Uh *huh*," I said to myself, "I see. All right." The next time I played the scene just as written without adding an iota of imagination to help it along. We went through that day, *and* the next day, in the same fashion. I did nothing more than say the words and do action only as required in the dialogue. On the third day, Darryl Zanuck appeared. He asked me what the matter was, and I said, "Nothing."

"Come on, now. There is something the matter."

"No, no. I'm just doing it as required. I'm playing the script just as written."

"Now, that isn't what we *want*," Zanuck said, in unconscious revelation. "Get with it, boys."

He left the set, and next day the director came in nice as pie, and there was no further trouble. This director and I became good friends and we worked together several times after that without the slightest difficulty.

Direction, I've always held, is implicit in the writing. One doesn't go to the post with a bad script if he can help it. If the script is right, the direction is all there, implicit in the writing. Consequently, whenever I hear much ranting and roaring about this, that, or the other great director, I will admit there are some directors who are imaginative, who can get the most out of their material. Hawks, Wellman, Walsh, Keighley, Curtiz, Del Ruth, Ford, and others were all expert and did their job to the fullest. But many directors are just pedestrian workmen, mechanics. Ostensibly they choose camera angles and on occasion they do, but I've often seen cameramen take over when needed. The director would indicate where he wanted it, and quietly the cameraman would indicate to his assistant a spot one good foot off the director's mark. Then the cameraman would turn to me, wink, and walk away.

There are some directors I've seen, and with great reputations, who couldn't direct you to a cheap delicatessen. One fella, a faker of the first order, developed a highly workable technique to impress the front office. Having at least the shrewdness to get a best seller for a start and the best actors available, he'd let them do all the work, and fine work it would be. Then, to associate himself tangibly with all this, this "director" as the cameras were turning would walk into the set and say, "All right, now come on, kids—give me lots of heart!" Then he'd turn around, walk out, and say, "Action." The action promptly ensued, and very good action it would be. Then, just before he said "Cut," he strolled back into the scene again to say, "All right, that's fine. Very good scene. You gave me everything I needed, kids. Just what I wanted. Cut!" The big bosses would look at these rushes with this gentleman's self-serving little prologue and epilogue, and come to the conclusion that he was quite a guy. This man, by the way, who was in my view a distinct failure as a director, failed himself right into a fortune. He, too, was wonderful. Negatively—but wonderful.

Like him, many of these so-called directors just stood by and watched. In some cases, it was because the person they were filming would have to be in complete charge in any case. Who, for example, would tell Freddie Astaire where to go in any of his dance numbers? Once I visited him on the set, and just after I arrived, the director yelled "Cut!" in the middle of a dance, and walked over to talk with Freddie. I thought this odd, and at lunch I said so, asking Freddie if the director had ever done this before. "No," said Freddie. "Pretty strange, isn't it?" I got the distinct flavor of the director showing off for the visiting fireman.

The best movie I made overseas was, fittingly enough, one with an Irish locale. It is not hard to be objective about the beauty of Ireland: it speaks unarguably for itself. *Shake Hands with the Devil* (1959), an account of the 1921 "Troubles," was made memorable for me by shooting it at Bray in the beautiful countryside close to Dublin. Getting to know and love that lush greenness, I was appalled a few years later to read that rural Ireland stood in danger of being mined and industrialized. I sent on to the Irish *Times* a few words capsulating my reaction to that chilling news, but not identifying myself. I used the pseudonym of Harley Quinn—Harlequin.

> You want to see the Shannon like the Hudson
> Or the Liffey just as filthy as the Seine?
> Bring in the arrogant asses
> And their garbage and their gasses—
> The pollutants plunging poison down each drain:
> Killing everything that's living
> For which nature's unforgiving,
> And the punishment will certainly fit the crime.
> Where man, the creeping cancer,
> Will have to make the final answer
> As he smothers 'neath his self-created slime.

I don't know if they ever published it, but fortunately my apprehensions vanished with the news later that the Irish Government had canceled the impending mining contracts. Practical foresight.

In 1960, Bob Montgomery and I got together to do *The Gallant Hours,* a labor of love, a tribute to that wonderful man, Admiral William F. "Bull" Halsey. Bob as co-producer and director deliberately steered away from big battle scenes and roaring guns. We concentrated on Halsey himself, trying to convey some of the tensions of high command.

One Halsey incident put me strongly in mind of all the young people I grew up with. After a big battle where Halsey had sailed with all his ships right through the Japanese fleet, he did so in face of the most potential danger any navy was ever in. But he came out victoriously. At a board of inquiry later, when he was asked just why he endangered everything he had, he gave an absolutely great answer. He said, "One goes in with what one has, doesn't he?" That was the heart of the story of the young people I grew up with: they were going in with what they had. Sometimes it worked; sometimes it didn't. And the same thing applied to people in this very chancy show business—going in with what one has is just about the entire story. I've watched really talented people do that and then drop by the wayside. It's saddening because they were really so very talented, but perhaps there was lacking a fullness of that competitive instinct needed to hold one's own in this high-risk business.

Deep down, of course, in show people, in *all* people, is that basic drive for recognition, for identification with something of value. In preparing the Halsey story we came across the incident of a chief petty officer on leave who got drunk. The Shore Patrol caught up with him, and by that time he was in very rough shape, a falling-down drunk. The Shore Patrol asked him what ship he belonged to. The sailor didn't identify the ship; he didn't identify his unit. All he said—with great pride—was, "I'm one of Halsey's men." How true of us all; to be a part of the best is everybody's search.

In order to publicize our movie of Halsey, this remarkable man, I had the opportunity to meet two more. I was given the chance to do a brief television appearance with Gene Tunney and Jack Dempsey. Again, two of our very much-needed heroes, two wonderfully charming gentlemen. Just like my encounter with Babe Ruth and Roger Bresnahan, I got goose pimples meeting these two giants of the fight ring. Rehearsing for this television spot was solid laughter.

There were inevitably the traditional poses of Tunney thrusting his fist out and Dempsey crouching in reaction, and as Tunney did so, Dempsey said to him, "You're not going to stick *that* thing in my nose again, are you?" As we were rehearsing our little scene together, we read our lines off the TelePrompTer, and my glasses weren't doing much for me. Neither, apparently, were Tunney's. We both called out, "Closer, closer." Dempsey, on the other hand, could see a gnat at twenty paces, so when Tunney finally said, "I still can't see it!," Dempsey countered with, "You guys can't see; I can't read!"

Before I began my next picture, *One, Two, Three*, I had no forewarning that it would be my last. It was not an easy picture to do because it was unrelieved comedy, a "be funny or else" affair that demanded unrelenting drive throughout. As I've said, comedy unadorned has never attracted me especially. When Billy Wilder gave me the script for *One, Two, Three*, its foreword said in effect, "We are embarking on a job here that requires sixty around the curves, and a hundred miles per hour on the straightaway." I can see why he thought of me. I've been a rat-a-tat talker all my life. But when we went at it, it verified for me that speed is always relative. Something is fast only because something else is slower.

In shooting a scene as I was going along at a hell of a clip, Wilder asked me if I had ever played anything this fast before. I said yes, *Boy Meets Girl*, which Warner's had bought for Pat O'Brien and me. Even in 1938 when we made it, Pat and I had been around many a day, and we knew the absolute need for pacing, letting air in at certain spots to prevent it from being unadulterated rush. We fought the Warner's brass on this, and at the points where they won, the results for the picture were sad. I explained this to Wilder, and he said, "My God, don't frighten me."

"No," I said, "but let's benefit from experience. Let's take our time for a spiel, then pick it up and go like hell again." And this is what we did to a degree. I never saw the picture, but they tell me it was funny. I hope so. It was certainly a lot of hard work.

It is very interesting that not until the very end of my career did I meet an unco-operative fellow actor. As I review the pictures I've been in, I realize that each and every actor I worked with had a part in shaping my summary views on acting. We all worked together rewardingly with what I hope was mutual enrichment. I never had the slightest difficulty with a fellow actor until the making of *One, Two, Three*. In that picture, Horst Buchholz tried all kinds of scene-stealing didoes, and I had to depend on Billy Wilder to take some steps to correct this kid. If Billy hadn't, I was going to knock Buchholz on his ass, which at several points I would have been very happy to do.

In such nice contrast to this character was Pamela Tiffin, the ingenue in the picture. Here is living illustration of a point I have often made. The movies keep looking for new talent but so frequently fail to utilize the talent they have. In *One, Two, Three*, Pamela showed a remarkable flair for comedy, and as far as I know that is the only opportunity she was given. It is so rare to find a beautiful girl who can play comedy well. Carole Lombard, Kay Kendall, Lucille Ball, and you've just about gone down the roster. Because of sheer neglect, talents like Pamela Tiffin never come to their majority.

Retirement comes automatically to most people: age sixty-five, so many years on the job, ill health, whatever. For me retirement came easily and without premeditation. Shortly after it came, my sister, Jeannie, who is a close friend of Bob Hope's wife, was talking to Bob about it one day.

"Jeannie," Bob said, "how in the name of God can he do it? How can he retire after thirty years in pictures and forty years in show business?"

"What you don't know, Bob," she said, "is that Jim has been getting ready for this for thirty years."

"What do you mean?"

"Well, he bought his first farm in 1936, and he's been going there every summer and spending six months. So this is nothing new for him. He's been getting ready for it all that time."

As indeed I was. Bob is a remarkable man, year after year going on with all the enthusiasm he had at the start, all that talent in perpetual high gear. He told Jeannie he could never retire, and of course that is understandable. A fella learns his trick and does it over the years with ever-increasing expertness. He's not going to give it up easily. But acting was always a second choice with me; I was always aiming at the farm. Not long ago I drove down Ventura Boulevard past Warner Brothers where I made over forty of my sixty-two movies, and I didn't turn a hair. It didn't interest me one damn. In thinking about all my reasons for quitting, I can boil them down to one: when I stopped caring, I stopped acting.

I can almost pinpoint the moment it all stopped for me. Now, this moment was not the cause, it was just the occasion, the moment when I realized that I was going to pack it in. I was in Munich, making *One, Two, Three*. During my stay there, I had given my boat to Rolie Winters, who is also a good sailor man, to use over the summer because I knew he enjoyed it. On this particular day, I had just received a letter from him with a picture enclosed. The photo was of Rolie and his wife and of a number of other friends sitting in the boat raising their glasses to the camera and me. At the bottom of the picture Rolie had written, "Nice you are gainfully employed!"

As I looked at the photo I savored their enjoyment. At least for this one moment I was sharing some of their pleasure: I was out in the sun, and the green was green as green, and the air was clean. I was experiencing this part of my day with pleasure. Then the assistant director came and said, "Mr. Cagney, we are ready." So inside the studio I went, and as they closed the giant doors behind me and I found myself in that great black cavern with just a few spotlights dotted here and there, I said to myself, "Well, this is it. This is the end. I'm finished."

I knew at that moment that I would never bother about acting any more. It was the logical conclusion of my long-continuing,

26. With brother Bill, prime business advisor and life long chum.

27. Cagney at rest . . .

28. . . . at exercise . . .

29. . . . at sail . . .

deeply felt instinct to separate myself from all the stresses I had found in the picture business. I had always put as much distance between those stresses and myself as I possibly could. Now came the inevitable ending. After *One, Two, Three* was completed, I didn't even bother to see the picture, and I don't think I ever will. All this for the simplest of reasons: I'm just not that much interested. I had the career—it was fine, I enjoyed it, but it was over.

℃ 11 ℂ

After a lifetime spent as an actor, I would be odd indeed if I didn't have a few thoughts about my profession. In talking to Pamela Tiffin about it all once, I think I summed up a few of my basic positions. I told her that for me acting begins with an awareness that the *audience* is why I'm doing what I'm doing. I'm acting for them, not for myself, and I do it as directly as I can. Arthur Johnson, the stepfather of my good friend Albert Hackett, was D. W. Griffith's leading man in the old Biograph days, and a first-rate actor he was. A tall, lank man with a commanding mane of hair, he looked as if he had authority, and he acted as if he had it, too. He gave his stepson some acting advice, which in turn was passed along to me, advice that I treasure. Johnson's advice on how to play a scene was affirmative: "You walk in, and plant yourself squarely on both feet, and then say what you have to say." I remembered that.

When we were making *One, Two, Three,* I told Pamela Tiffin that because we had an awful lot of things to say to each other in our first scene, it would help if we got our heads together and talked it over. She agreed, and as we worked on the scene I noticed she just couldn't look me in the eye. Self-conscious, ill at ease. I wanted to help a bit.

"Want to listen to a minute of old-man talk?"

"What is it?"

"Rule 1."

"What's that?"

"You walk in, plant yourself, look the other fella in the eye, and tell the truth." She asked me to repeat it, and I did. I told her the source of that advice, and I explained my little addition to Johnson's sound instruction: "I also tell you, 'Look the other fella in the eye and tell the truth' because you weren't looking at me." So may I say, bless her, she did just that, never wavering for a moment.

In a later scene, however, her eyes did begin to wander again. But this is quite common among inexperienced players. They glance from your left eye to your right eye almost in Ping-Pong fashion.

"One more thing," I told her. "Look in the downstage eye."

"Which one is that?"

"The one nearest the camera." Which is what she did thereafter.

The best kind of authentic talent has a fundamental quality that I can only identify as courage. Be it boxing, baseball, or acting, the ones who come up through the ranks—the Dempseys, MacFarlands, Ruths, Barrymores—all need courage in great degree, because without it, they couldn't endure those rough, tough conditions. When these champions began their life work there were no guarantees of any kind. Not like today where, to use that stupid and ridiculous word, a superstar is created overnight. When the champions I admired began their working life there was no unemployment insurance, or other aids. If they had no job, they were on the borrow, trying to patch their way from one engagement to another.

The Barrymores were fascinating. I had contact with them just a few times. On a radio broadcast of J. M. Barrie's *The Old Lady Shows Her Medals* for the Motion Picture Relief Fund, Lionel Barrymore played J. M. Barrie, Ethel played the old lady, and I did the young soldier in the piece. In talking to her beforehand, I said, "What accent are you going to use, Miss Barrymore?," intending to follow her lead.

"You are listening to it, James. You are listening to it!" she said in that thrillingly resonant Barrymore tone.

When the Screen Actors Guild honored Lionel on one of his birthdays, as Guild president, I had to make the presentation. It was a pleasure to meet this completely charming old gentleman, and his courage was evident in the fact of his total naturalness. Despite the wheelchair and his crippling arthritis, there were no apologies or implied need for sympathy.

As to the youngest of the Barrymores, he had courage in his own way. Never wanting to be an actor, John was forced to go on the stage by his family, thereby frustrating his desire to become an artist. He had to continue with the theatre and Hollywood because he knew no other profession. It was the sad story of a man who could not do what he wanted with his life, but even in his last sad days of alcoholic self-parody, he complained to no man. One evening I was in the Brown Derby with Ed McNamara and Sidney Skolsky. We were in the end booth by the door when I heard a hissing sound coming to us from four or five booths down. Ed was on the outside of the booth, so he stuck his head out and looked down toward the source of this odd sound. Then we could hear the words, plain and clear: "Piss-ant, piss-ant!"

McNamara saw who it was and said, "It's Jack Barrymore. He's saying 'Piss-ant!,' and I think he means you, Cagney."

"Well, we'll find out," I said, and I walked down to the Barrymore booth. I had never met him, but I came up and said, "You sent for me?"

"Yes, I sent for you."

"What have I done?"

"That's just it. It's what you *haven't* done. Play it, goddamn it, play it!"

"Play what?"

"*The Playboy of the Western World*. You were born to play it. Play it! Goddamn it, why don't you do it?"

"Well, nobody ever asked me."

"Oh, so that's the kind of piss-ant you are!"

This little episode points up a key aspect of my grounded view toward acting. For the big roles, the classics—I just never had any interest. I've known any number of actors who have always yearned to play the big roles, and as much as I applaud that kind of dream, I never had it for myself.

Indeed, my aim was never stardom. I never gave it a thought in my early years, and after I was given the designation, I didn't think about it then. With me, a career was the simple matter of putting the groceries on the table. I've never thought of myself as anything but a journeyman actor, going where the job happened to be, doing the job, and making my way back home. I see youngsters these days specifically program themselves to be stars in a set time period. This surely is a mistake. One shouldn't aspire to stardom, one should aspire to be doing the job well.

But, and how vital this is, if you don't have the inborn quality the audience buys, you will get nothing, or very little. You can be a very limited actor like Errol Flynn in his early days and still make it because of that quality the audience wants. Errol developed flair and technique as the years went by, but he always had that quality people bought at the box office.

One lady I knew briefly, a former European star, speaking of my career, said to me, "You must be very proud, Mr. Cagney."

"I'm not."

"Why?"

"Because I had nothing to do with it. If whatever I had to sell was acceptable to the audience, where did it come from? You can't take bows for your having red hair, you can't take bows for having blue eyes. The things I am were passed on to me from someone else. It doesn't necessarily follow that the fella who makes the big splash ever did anything on his own."

"But such a man exerted himself; he had to extend himself," the lady replied.

"Yes," I said, "but where did that capacity for extension come from? Did *he* generate the thing? Not at all. It was *there*."

Not long after this discussion, I read a biography of that

tremendous artist and human being, Charlie Russell. Of his work he said, "I count myself lucky. I happened to have the ability to put stuff on canvas, or to do it in clay, or whatever, but I had nothing to do with it. I had it to start with, and where it came from, who knows? But I happened to be able to put it together and make a living with it." Russell summed it all up: "Cash in my checks now. I've been a lucky man." Yes. So I say about my long years of work.

Undue self-concern is tied into this. Unremitting self-interest can only hurt one. During the making of a picture directed by Charlie Vidor, I noticed him come into the studio one morning looking very low and disconsolate. I asked him what the matter was.

"Ah, Jimmy, everybody hurt me, everybody hurt me."

"How do you mean, hurt you?"

"They say things. I don't think they mean to hurt me, but they do. They say really cruel things, and it weighs on me the whole day."

"Do you want to get rid of that, Charlie? Well—just ask yourself one question and the hurt will disappear *that* fast. The question is this: just ask yourself, 'Who the hell do I think I am?' And you'll see the hurt will disappear."

"Ah, Jimmy, I can't do that."

"Why not?"

"Because I think I'm somebody."

And with that view, inevitably, comes insecurity and frustration and unhappiness.

To me the very essence of show business is change, variety— and one often very neglected and little-touted element: idiocy. I remember saying to a particularly beautiful actress, "Look, pet, you are intelligent; God knows you're beautiful. Everything about you is fine. There might be just one thing lacking: you don't have that very necessary quality of idiocy."

On this idiocy matter, my old chum Rolie Winters and I have aphorized the word to come up with a favorite expression, "God Bless Idiocy." We find that most of our laughs derive from some ridiculous thing he or I said or heard. After forty years we still get a chuckle from the classic show business story of one actor meeting a fellow thespian on Broadway. The first actor says, "Oh, I tell you, when I went over to Campbell's Funeral Parlor and you were bidding goodbye to your wife—well, I want to tell you—in all my life I've never seen anybody so affected, hit so hard by the loss of a loved one."

"At Campbell's Funeral Parlor?"

"Yes, that's where I saw you."

"Oh, hell, that was nothing. You should have caught me at the grave!"

That kind of unbounded and artless egoism is almost endearing in its idiocy. And yet there is one part of the story that hits the truth: you're only as good as the other fella thinks you are. The reason for that is simple. He buys the tickets. In any aspect of creativity one would care to name, the one who thinks he has all the answers is finished, through as of that moment. One time my artist friend Ralph Armstrong was on the set. We'd just finished a shot, but I looked at the director and said, "Let's go again." We did it again. Afterward, Ralph said, "What was wrong with the first one?" I said I wasn't sure, it just wasn't any good. Ralph said it looked good to him, but I told him that if something says, "Look out. It's no good," one better listen to that little voice.

"It seems to me, Jim," Ralph said, "that if you've been doing it for as long as you have, that when you do it, it's right." I had to explain to Ralph again that one must at least be sure when one's not right. As soon as you're *sure* about everything in acting, I told him, you're through. "I really mean it," I told him. "When you're positive you've got all the answers, you haven't got any answers that are worth anything."

"I don't know about that," Ralph said.

At that time Ralph had great success with his painting. He was a good craftsman, drew superbly, and his pastels of perfectly beautiful gals were showpieces that the magazines bought avidly. Then the magazine world started to diminish, and Ralph had rather a rough time thereafter. It may well be, too, that a man who is sure that everything he does is right is really not going to be able to stay the course.

Years ago in the theatre there was, among a number of actor classifications, the interesting one of the so-called office actor. He was the one who would go to a casting office to try out for a particular role and in the *office* give one hell of a convincing performance, impressing both producer and director very much. This ability, however, would not extend to the stage when he was actually doing the part. Some essential part of him would wither up when he was before an audience. In direct contrast to him would be the actor—frequently Milquetoastish in demeanor—who had no "office" presence at all but who could, once on stage, astonish everyone with the power of his playing.

A case in point was William B. Mack, who played Joe Gerson, the self-sacrificing murderer in *Within the Law* on Broadway many years ago. Nobody meeting Mack, a picture of diffidence, would ever have guessed that he was connected even remotely with show business. He had great difficulty obtaining work in the theatre because he simply was unable to give an "office" performance. Finally, when Holbrook Blinn cast Mack in *Within the Law*, it was something of a Broadway revolution. Mack, instead of doing the traditional heavy-breathing, glary-eyed villain, did it gently, speaking softly. All by himself, he set a new pattern for heavies, even interspersing some humor. It's a brand of acting I particularly admire—to the point, non-arty.

There is, of course, an aspect of acting that gets its share of notice in print and elsewhere and that is the "art" of it. To begin with my bailiwick, our pictures at Warner's were programmers created purely to satisfy the need of many thousands of theatres and their weekly and frequently semiweekly double-feature bills. Not long ago, Freddie Astaire was in New York to receive an honor, and during the course of it he was asked a number of questions. At one point his interviewers spoke at some length about the art of his dancing. Freddie stopped them cold in their tracks.

"What do you mean—art?" he said. "Art—my foot! It was just hard, hard work. I broke my back getting those routines done, did everything that was necessary, and the only art in it was work. If it appeared like art, so much the better, but believe me, it was pure labor." Freddie said it all. Acting is work, nothing more or less than work, and it comes into existence only *with* work.

As to any overall Cagney theory of acting, I think back to about 1925, when I had been a professional actor only a short time. I was asked by some people to come down to talk to their drama class. I was supposed to tell these youngsters what I knew about acting and what my theories were. When I stood before them, I said I didn't know anything about it really. I just made my living at it. On reflection, that seems to have been my philosophy all the way through.

I realize there is a great deal of theorizing about acting. There are those who speak of the subjective viewpoint, others who speak of the objective viewpoint, and all kinds of shadings between. My personal feeling is simply this: the meaning of acting is implicit in the word itself. Acting means acting, *action*—and I'm constantly amazed by the behavior of young people today who take up screen time just being there. I'd add only one other thing to these things I've been saying about acting from my point of vantage: you should quit when you're psychologically finished.

Jim Jeffries once got up in the ring at Hollywood Regents Stadium after a very fulsome introduction. He said his few words and added, "Well, boys and girls, I think I'll quit while I'm still standing." Surely that's the best, the *only* way to quit. For the ones who hang on hoping it's all going to strike again—no. It never does.

Upon retirement, I soon found that there weren't enough hours in the day. When one begins to give full time to beauty in all its myriad forms, the hours close in. I cannot ever remember not being moved, and I mean most deeply, by beauty. Once I was looking at the charming ballet dancer, Harriet Hoctor. Instead of landing from one of her ascents, she settled to the ground like some ethereal bird. Watching her, I burst suddenly into tears, not loudly but enough for my wife to know something had happened to her old man. She asked me what the matter was and I said,

"I'm sorry. It's just that this thing hit me." But I cry at horse races, footraces—anything where I'm looking at total effort. It just hits me in the center and I cry.

I have always appreciated art; whether I could create it or not is open to question. Certainly I can recall in my preschool years copying out of the newspapers, just drawing pictures of shoes and clothing and people the way kids will. One art teacher in grammar school around 1911 took us to the Metropolitan Museum of Art, where for the first time I beheld the work of that great American master, Thomas Eakins, and in particular his painting "The Thinker," a man standing with hands in pockets, looking at the ground. I haven't seen that painting since, but I've never forgotten it.

Over the years I've done caricatures of my friends, and when I toured Army hospitals in Europe during the war, I would do caricatures of the wounded kids on their plaster casts in the hope that that would amuse them momentarily at least. Then in the late 1950s I was with my old friend Jack Bailey in a restaurant. Across the aisle from us was a youngster with an interesting face, which I drew. Jack asked me how long I had been doing that, and I admitted it had been for a span of years. He asked me why I didn't do something about it, and the next day he made sure I did.

He arrived at our house with a box full of paints and canvas. In time he introduced me to his teacher, Sergei Bongart, a Russian from Kiev—a great painter, a great human being. I've rejoiced both in his tutelage and his friendship. My lessons with him are highly beneficial, although I must confess that during them we talk more than we paint.

When I first came to Sergei, he thought I was just another actor dilettante. He asked me if I was serious, and on receiving emphatic assurance on the point, he began his very interesting teaching process. He drew a square on a piece of cardboard and divided it into four different-shaded parts. "There," he said, "are your four values: light, halftone, dark, and black. Now, this is what you are going to do first. You're going to do a still life in black and white."

To be able to see the values in stark black and white is quite a trick, and I worked on that for two months, producing some of the most horrendous things ever to sully a canvas. But I kept after my homework, and one day I flashed a still life on him that, heart-warmingly, he applauded. It was the first thing I ever did that he labeled as professional, and this led on to the next plateau: color. Once again I churned out some lively horrors, but gradually I began to come up with some meaningful relationships of form, color, and perspective. I think the first thing I learned is that although certain skills are attained and stay with one, you never have all the answers. You keep plugging away trying to learn something.

Since childhood, a certain fella has been on my mind. This is the fighter who goes through his career as a terrific puncher but also as a terrific receiver. He winds up with a flat nose; cauliflower ears; thick, protrusive lips; proud flesh over his eyes; cuts on the cheekbone; slashes around his mouth—a human caricature. I've seen these fellas come out of fights with everything hanging loose—ears, lips, eyes—but victorious. This kind of guy has stayed in my mind for years. I have been making sketches of him with arm held high by the referee although his legs are folding under him; his eyes are almost sightless from the pounding—but still he stands, a battered hulk, victorious. From these sketches I did an oil painting I call "The Winner" and took it into Bongart.

"Jesus Christ, Jimmy! Who's that?"

"I've been thinking of this poor guy. He's numbered by the thousands in the fight racket."

"Very spooky, very spooky."

And infinitely sad as well. When I did the fight movies I always used the smallest gloves we could get. They would cut, but I'd much rather be cut than have a concussion headache for twenty-four hours or longer. For years I've been advocating total removal of gloves for fighters. With bone against bone, flesh against flesh, they would, for example, hit somebody on top of the head with the bare fist just once. Thereafter they'd become sharpshooters or body punchers, aiming at vulnerable points with considerably less danger involved. I've always contended this is the only way to stop boys dying in the ring from cerebral hemorrhages.

I remember a boy being killed this way at the Olympic Stadium in Los Angeles. I told my friend, Jim Richardson, then city editor of the Los Angeles *Examiner*, that he really should start a campaign to take the gloves off those kids. I explained to him that it was the damned glove that caused those murderous concussions. After determining that I was perfectly serious about this, Richardson assigned his sports editor to interview me over the phone. This goddamned clown evidently thought I was looking for publicity because he made a joke of the entire thing. He said, "I expect to hear any day now that Cagney's going to do a new fight picture called *The Return of Jim Plague, Bare-knuckle Fist Fighter.*" This little witticism reached the public a few days before a boy in an amateur bout, wearing a headguard, was killed in a Los Angeles ring.

I have long cherished a bronze pair of fighters, a sculpture with an interesting history. Before these two were cast, they were in wax model form—the work, I hoped and believed, of Charles Russell. If they were from his hands, it was the only non-Western piece he ever did. I bought this model from a chap named Britsman, a biographer of Russell's, who had been in contact with Russell and his wife over the years. Britsman gave me the opportunity to subscribe to a projected casting of a number of Russell's Western pieces. Almost to one side in the mass of material Britsman had collected was this wax model of two fighters in combat. The model was unsigned, hence its authenticity as a Russell was very moot. Because I've been interested in fighters all my life, I was attracted to it, and Mr. Britsman told me to take it, saying he had no use for it. Appreciatively, I kept the fighters through many years, but of course, being wax, they began to deteriorate, and I realized they should be cast for preservation.

Authentication was a difficult business, however. Then one evening on television I saw Milburn "Doc" Stone, talking with real assurance on Russell paintings. I got in touch with Milburn, whom I did not then know, and during a pleasant evening together he told me about Frederick Renner, who is *the* expert on Russells. Renner was able to come out to see my wax model, and he said that even though there was no signature, it was undoubtedly a Russell. At the same time he explained that he couldn't authenticate it officially because if, in the very faint likelihood that it turned out to be a fraud, he, Renner, would be held responsible for misauthentication. This I quite understood. He told me to get in touch with Joe de Young, an old friend of Russell's, who was himself a sculptor/painter. Perhaps Joe could help me.

I took the model to Joe. Joe is deaf and, interestingly, although he can speak, he always writes down what he wants to communicate. When Joe saw the model, he smiled broadly, looked at me, and reached for his pencil. He wrote, "I was there when he did it." I had always wondered who the two fighters might be, and I asked Joe. Joe said he was in Shelby, Montana, when Russell did the model in July 1923, and the fighters were Jack Dempsey and Tommy Gibbon, who had fought a memorable heavyweight championship bout there that month. Joe said he watched Russell craft the piece, and it was from Joe that I obtained written authentication that I did indeed own an original Russell. I had it cast in bronze and now it lives forever, gladdening my heart and the heart of anyone who sees it.

The reality and life I see in Russell, Beierstadt, Remington, and all the other great Western painters is literally glorious, and I am much amused by the boys who have condemned them as corny. The wise boys in the critical hierarchy have recently elected Andrew Wyeth, that solidly, richly human painter, as the current corny one. To me such nonsense points up the essential bankruptcy of those who throw out the rules. One works or plays without rules at real peril to function, and when in art I see abstract and non-representational work that defies the sound basis of painting aesthetics, I know that I am looking at nonsense, and pretty pretentious nonsense at that. There isn't a human endeavor you can name—baseball, government, boxing, education—in which common-sense rules aren't essential and profitable. If one freewheels his way as total self-arbiter, one loses one's way.

One thinks of Fauvism. Les Fauves (The Wild Beasts) were young French painters at the beginning of this century who revolted against nature as a source of art's truth. A fundamental rule in painting, many centuries old, is that in exterior landscaping the light is warm, the shadow cool; in an interior, of course, the shadows are warm, the light is cool. This is so because it is inevitably a north light used to light up the subject. The Fauves, however, changed the rules to suit themselves, and one can see their heritage in modern abstract art, with its consequent burden of chaos. In this nonsense I see nothing to intrigue the eye or the heart—which in my view is what art is all about. As to what art is *not* about, there are, among others, the works of Picasso, which I consider glamorous chunks of garbage, daubs of brilliant, uninhibited fakery.

A very practical instance of the need for rules was the Dempsey-Willard fight in 1919, which I saw on film not long ago. Dempsey beat Willard very badly, and as he knocked him down, Dempsey stood over Willard, waiting for him to rise and continue. The film's commentary was interesting for what it didn't say. Evidently the people who put the film together didn't realize that they were witnessing the last prize fight ever that allowed the man who knocks a fighter down to stand over his victim. It was just after this fight that the rule of the neutral corner was instituted, the rule that requires a fighter after making a knockdown to go to a neutral corner before the referee begins the count. By an interesting irony, it was this very rule that cost Jack his championship. Seven years later, when he was fighting Gene Tunney, Dempsey knocked him to the canvas and completely forgot the neutral-corner rule. The referee had to stop and insist that Dempsey go to a far corner, and by the time the count was started there was enough delay for Tunney to gather his strength and come back to win. The neutral-corner rule was necessary because it made a prize fight a genuine contest rather than a primitive exhibition. It is another verification that rules are essential in keeping order in any sort of effort.

In defining art, one can't do better, I believe, than citing the view of William Ernest Hocking, professor emeritus of philosophy at Harvard, who wrote the stimulating book *The Strength of Men and Nations*. I have heard many definitions of art, but Professor Hocking's seems to me the best. Art, he says, is life— plus caprice. Thus, a simple declarative statement grows into a Shakespearean line, or several notes brought together become the theme of a Brahms symphony. Caprice, that element over and above life itself, operating under the artist's structured guidance, creates beauty where before there was only ordinariness.

Caprice, of course, is an undefinable thing, summoned whence no one knows, creating its own kind of tensions. Patricia Steinke, a fine painter, wrote kiddingly of her feelings when facing a virgin canvas:

> Whenever I see a canvas stretchéd
> It makes me feel, oh, so wretched!

I wrote her back:

> You felt what others were made to feel:
> Rembrandt, Homer, and Charley Peale
> When they face the pallid, tortured tightness
> A need to impose a divuséd brightness—
> That need strong part of the artist's store
> To create a life where was none before.

My bent for art has been obvious since early childhood, and if my father and mother had been more aware of it all those long years ago, it would probably have been well if they had steered me in that direction. I might not have been as materially successful as I was in show business, but, taking it all in all, I might have been a lot happier.

I can't leave the subject without hearkening back to my introduction to active art tutelage through the agency of Jack Bailey. Jack, for so many years the master of ceremonies for "Queen for a Day," is a remarkable fella. A former alcoholic, he has been an AA activist for over two decades, and besides his work there he has studied trombone, the piano, and music in general. He is a serious artist, in addition, and does an excellent job there too. I was talking to another old friend, Ralph Wheelwright, about this many-sided man. I told Ralph of how Bailey would do his daily show, take his wife out to dinner, go to an AA meeting or an art lesson or a trombone lesson or a piano lesson. And to top all these accomplishments off, Bailey made his own picture frames and stretched his own canvases. I detailed to Ralph just how tremendous a fella Bailey was and how dedicated he was to living.

Some time later Ralph was walking into a Beverly Hills art shop, and who should be walking out but Jack Bailey, arms full of manufactured blank canvases. As it happened, Ralph knew Jack by sight, but Jack didn't know Ralph. Ralph, I must explain, has a very cold blue eye, and his myopia requires him to wear thick glasses. With this intimidating appearance in his favor, he stopped Jack dead in the door with the words, "Mr. Bailey, I must say this. I *must* say this. You, sir, are a liar and a fraud."

"I don't know what you mean," said Jack, properly stunned by this style of address from a total stranger.

"Yes, you know what I mean. A good friend of yours—and I mean a very good friend—has been boasting to me about you as long as I've known him: what a remarkable man you are, how you do this, do that, and among other things how you make your own frames and stretch your own canvas. Yet here you are, coming out of a shop with your arms full of everything he described to me as homemade. And I repeat to you, sir, that you are a liar and a fraud."

"Just a minute," Jack said. "Who said this?"

"A very good friend."

"Exactly who is this good friend?"

"Jim Cagney."

After taking a beat, Jack said, "He's an actor, isn't he?"

"Yes."

"He's an Irishman, isn't he?"

"That's correct."

"Well, the truth isn't in him!" And with that, Jack clutched his canvases in his arms and ran out of the store.

~ 12 ~

Not long ago I was at a party where I met a young actor, a charming fella, seemingly confident and well-poised, a pleasure to talk to. Unexpectedly, he asked me if I had ever been in therapy.

"No."

"Never?"

"Never."

"Why's that?"

"Why should I be?"

"Well," he said, "everybody I know has been in therapy at one time or another."

"Not I."

"I don't understand it."

I tried to help him understand by pointing out that I was too busy trying to keep the groceries on the table to take time out to lie down on anybody's couch. After having had an awful lot of early jolts, when another came along I was able to shrug my shoulders and say, "Oh, what the hell." I have met so many people like that young man in our business who have spent so many precious and life-wasting hours on the psychiatrist's couch. I think people who do that are taking themselves too seriously and are just self-absorbed to the point where they are completely miserable. If they could just love something outside themselves, life would ease up for them. This self-absorption gives one an added and totally superfluous personality. Of course, at times an added personality is *externally* imposed. As I wrote of one (among many similar) Hollywood lady:

> She walks in a beauty so proudly paradable
> It's hard to believe that it's biodegradable.

Absorption in things other than self is the secret of a happy life, I'm sure. May I ramble on a bit about some of the absorptions of my later years? In addition to my love of the land, there is my love of the sea and for any ship under sail. I favor the traditional Chesapeake Bay bugeye. Years ago I saw a topsail schooner being built at the Crane Shipyard in Ipswich, Massachusetts. As I walked into the yard they were putting the decking on its classically beautiful hull, and I fell in love with this entrancing lady, a replica of the *Baltimore Clipper*. After she was launched, I kept track of her until a point when she was in Florida; thereafter I couldn't trace her.

A bit later I was cruising around Newport Beach Harbor with Spence Tracy in a little putt-putt, and I looked up to behold the *Swift of Ipswich*, my beautiful topsail schooner. They had brought her out to the West Coast to sell. At that time I had an old standard-type schooner, the *Martha*, eighty-six feet overall and about fifty-six on the water line. She was a great old boat, launched in 1907, and she's still afloat, with full-length planking and not a butt in her anywhere. The *Martha* sailed like a dream, and I certainly didn't need or want another one. But the little motion picture company we had at the time was contemplating filming the story of Port Royal, the infamous pirate city that disappeared beneath the sea presumably because it was the Sodom and Gomorrah of the Western world. I asked brother Bill to buy the *Swift of Ipswich* because it would fit beautifully into any such story of the sea.

But not long after we bought the boat, Paramount did a big pirate epic, *Frenchman's Creek*, and shortly after, Bob Hope did *The Princess and the Pirate*, in which he kidded all pirate stories. All of this made it very inauspicious for us to do the picture, so it was dropped. However, we kept the *Swift* from 1941 to 1956, chartering it out to other companies who wanted a boat of that type. She was a very colorful vessel, and I loved her very much. When we sold her, because I hadn't anything to sail in the East I ordered a forty-three-foot Chesapeake Bay bugeye designed by Chapell, the man who created the *Swift*. This is a ketch rig job that sails in shallow waters, and it has been wonderful for me and for my friends and family. This boat draws only three feet, nine inches, and on the East Coast there are so many places she can put into, exciting little inlets that she can traverse comfortably.

It's a different story on the West Coast for sailing. There in conventional waters, when I used to sail to Catalina, down to San Diego, and up to Santa Barbara, I didn't have too much fun. I am inclined in any case to seasickness, and I never know when it's going to hit. I'll be out on a day when it's very rough and no sign of *mal de mer,* and then go out another day when the weather's not bad at all and I'll heave for hours. The West Coast sailing is predictable; in the East there is always the unknown beckoning just beyond the next headland.

In pondering the durable beauty of the land, it has always been a dream of mine to build a stone house with my own hands. On my New York farm I started to do just that with the guidance of Gerald W. Papendick—"Pappy" to me—who can build anything. Pappy, a builder and contractor and man of many talents, lives in Joshua Tree, California, but he comes to my place in Dutchess County and works there summers. When I designed the very simple house I live in, I got Pappy, who on top of everything else is an excellent stonemason, to give me moral support when I began to work. But, as it turned out, every time I went to pick up a stone to fit in a particular place, Pappy would say pleasantly, "No, not that one—*that* one." I had the talent for picking precisely the wrong stone every single time. He would pick the right one unerringly. I'm damned glad I deferred to him because the result is an interesting-looking house, simple, sturdy, no nonsense.

Our family always gets a good laugh when the newspapers talk about the Cagney "estate" in Dutchess County. Some people near us at the farm were astonished at the little house I have. "This guy's nuts," they said. "Why would Cagney build a house like this in a place like our area where it's all so plush and so very fancy?" The plain truth is I don't like plush houses, I don't like fancy houses. I like to be able to sit down and put up my feet whenever I feel like it. Big, handsome places to me are a burden. So my Bill and I live in our simple little place overlooking a six-acre lake, which was the reason I bought the farm in the first place.

I have always had a thing for horses from just about as far back as I can remember. When I was a tiny kid, a friend of my dad's named Jimmy Hogan drove a two-wheeled cart for Blank's Meat Store on Eightieth Street and First Avenue. As I was playing on the street, he would come along with his horse-drawn cart, put me on the seat next to him, and take me on the rest of his deliveries. His horse was a big gray, almost white, with a huge behind. That horse looked like a giant to me as it clop-clop-clopped along in front of us. I was absolutely enchanted, loving it totally, and from that time on I've had a love for horses that has really marked my life.

My mother and the family had been riding horse-drawn streetcars from childhood, of course, and so it was a very emotional experience for her, my grandmother, and for me when we took a ride in 1907 on the last horse-drawn cars that traveled First Avenue. There is a beauty and a gallantry about horses that I have always felt deeply. They have always been my first love among animals, and I am an animal lover. My favorite horse is the Morgan, so functional, so beautiful with that small head, dish nose, arched neck, short back, and broad chest. They are perfect as either a working horse or a family horse, and anybody can ride them or drive them. They have a turn of speed as needed, too. I have been raising them off and on for the past thirty years, and along the way getting into trotters and pacers for a bit, which proved a mistake. One time I bought an Arabian stud to cross and hopefully fine up the Morgan heads, but that didn't work either. Now I am content to just breed my Morgans and to love them. I don't kid myself that I'm in it to turn a buck. The unvarnished fact is that the happiness I get out of just being around animals is literally indescribable. Seeing a gallant horse on the turn giving everything in him to win can make me choke up.

Also I can exult inwardly just by looking at a herd of cattle in a field when I drive by. At one time I went into cattle in a rather big way. For some time I had been hearing of the fine attributes of the Scotch Highlander, so I asked Rolie Winters if he'd go with me to take a look at some of them in a place in Pennsylvania. At that time Rolie was willing to get on a train and go anywhere, so off we went to Pittsburgh, where we were met by a Colonel Stetler, who drove us out to a farm that he chose to call his ranch. The colonel, wearing a ten-gallon hat and the high-heeled boots, took us out to see the cattle.

Scotch Highlanders have long red hair, and the red was about the color of mine when I was younger. Moreover, their eyes are rather sleepy and droopy. Winters looked at the cows, looked at me, and said, "Are these beef cattle?"

"Yes," I said.

"That means you're going to kill them and eat them?"

"Yes."

"You can't do that."

"Why not?"

"Because they look like your relatives!"

I didn't buy any of the colonel's cattle, but later I discovered a Scotch Highland farm in western Massachusetts. From there I bought a bull and four breed heifers and shipped them to the Vineyard. They needed no help; with all the grass and water they had, they flourished. When I bought the New York farm I sent them there. Then from South Dakota I bought almost a hundred head of Western Scotch Highland cattle, and the reproduction rate was very good indeed. Came then time for marketing them, and I found to my great sorrow that there was no such thing as a lively interest in Scotch Highland cattle. I shipped some of their steaks down to Ralph Bellamy, then in a New York play, and he took a couple of them to a friend who ran a fancy steak house on Canal Street. The man ate one and said it was the best he'd ever tasted.

The Highland has a way of putting the marbling inside the beef without laying it in great layers on the outside, which the Hereford and the Angus do. Thus the marbling is in the Scotch Highland at an early age, giving it an extra deliciousness. At an arranged meeting, I met a man who was also a friend of Bellamy's, and he gave me something to consider.

"Mr. Cagney," he said, "you don't know me and I don't know you. But you're a good friend of Bellamy's, and that's good enough for me. Now, I'm a meat buyer for many of the plush restaurants in town, but I'm also a lawyer by trade. I buy beef on the side. And I want to give you some advice. When you take the beautiful hide off a cow, there's meat remaining, that's all. What the cattle looked like with the hide on interests no one. Butchered, they are just food. Now, I'm advising you to sell all those beautiful cattle of yours, and put your money in blue-chip stock, because this is going to be a losing game for you."

I thanked him very much, and he said he was happy to be of help if indeed he had. He had. On my return to the farm, I called the market men and made a deal with them to take all my herd— all, that is, except for about a dozen, because it is quite true they are beautiful animals, and they are mightily eye-pleasing as they graze on a rich green hillside.

In enjoying the farm and my retirement, I have had to be aware of the need to maintain my health against the encroachments of age as best I can. My doctor tells me that if I want to be as active in my eighties as I am now in my seventies, twenty pounds must go. My living pattern in general is exemplary, but I must confess to one really pernicious habit: a consuming, racking passion for root beer floats—*large size*. My prime way to keep fit is to get out the old dancing board. When I did *The West Point Story* I was fifty-one, and in that I did a number with sixteen boys with a finish calling for a lot of hard dancing. The last bit consisted of doing a knee slide from the back of the stage down to the apron. This is a pretty vigorous business. Unknown to me, while we were doing the number, Gregory Peck was behind the camera. We shot this exhausting number five times and Gregory, then in his early thirties and knowing my age, mumbled to himself, "My God, how does he do it?" But he knew only my age; he didn't know that having been a hoofer I was reasonably well equipped to go on.

After my brother Harry died suddenly in 1964, I realized that a definitive health check was in order, so I got one and a clean bill of health from a bright young doctor. He asked me afterward to come down to Good Samaritan Hospital for some special tests. It seems they were intrigued by the fact of a sixty-five-year-old being in such good shape, and they wanted to find out why, particularly in view of the fact that I had been a professional athlete —a dancer—for forty-five years. I don't know if they ever found out for sure why I have stayed in such a state for so long, but it surely has something to do with keeping active. At times, though, my Irish-Norwegian stubbornness has driven me to dangerous antics with my health. Many years ago I'd done something to my left arm, and bursitis came in with everything flying. One day I was sitting alone on the deck of my boat with the pain really taking off the top of my head. I was rocking back and forth in full-scale agony when I decided I'd had enough of it. "The *hell* with it," I said, and I got up and swung my arm twenty-five times one way, twenty-five times the other. Then I sat down. Interestingly, that did it. No more pain. When I told my doctor brothers about it, they were properly aghast. "Do you realize what you could have done?" they asked. I told them at that moment I didn't give a damn. In any case, I haven't had bursitis in that arm since.

Health, it seems to me, depends in many ways on being able to preserve one's sense of wonder, to maintain an interest in all of life. I remember years ago telling my children, Jim and Casey, how completely necessary it is never to lose one's sense of wonder, never to take things for granted, never to assume anything is commonplace. The alternative is disinterest, boredom. This can kill, and once I saw it happen.

A friend of mine was involved. In the words of someone who knew him, our friend was "dying out of it." This man was having trouble at home, and discouragements were building up. I could see it happening—the weight loss because of lack of appetite, the growing disinterest with life. I said to Ralph Bellamy, "Come on, we can't let this happen to him." Our friend was literally dying out of his whole life scheme. So Ralph and I went out, picked him up, took him for a long drive, made the talk, and told the jokes. Not long after, we did it again, once more in order to rekindle his interest in living. It didn't work. He died. The doctors couldn't find anything wrong with him; he no longer maintained an interest, and so he just finished living.

By contrast, there was another friend of mine, living in New Jersey, who had had several strokes and was in terminal condition. At the time I was in Goshen, New York, driving an exhibition race for the U. S. Savings Bond Drive. I heard that my pal in New Jersey was dying, so I drove down at once and I asked the nurse, a gal I'd known previously, how my friend was doing. "Well, it's all over, Jim," she said. "He's really bad. Unconscious." I asked if I could go in and she said there would be no harm.

So I walked in, and here was my old friend, lying there, with hiccups racking his body and the sweat just pouring off his body. Death was in the room. I stood at the end of the bed and called him, "Will?" No answer. "Will?"

"Mmmm?"

"It's Jim. Jim Cagney."

"Mmm-huh. Hello, Jim."

I started to talk. I told him about going to Goshen and driving the race and who I'd heard from recently and all the things I could think of that might interest him. Within a half hour or so, the hiccups had stopped, the sweat was over, and his right arm, which had been lying uselessly across his chest, was up behind his head. He was talking to me. Even with the slurred speech from the stroke, he talked and talked. It wasn't many days before he was up and around, and he lived four years longer. And all of this because an interest was started again, a connection with life was begun and sustained.

That interest and wonder in things comes in all forms and from every sector of life when it is stimulated. One would hardly expect young people of unique vision to emerge from my rough old neighborhood, but I think of the Torporcer boys among several of my old friends. There is George, who loved baseball but was afflicted with very poor vision. Notwithstanding, his interest in the game was so strong that it ultimately led to the big leagues, where he maintained a career batting average of about .295. They called him "Specs" for obvious reasons, and the gallant perseverance of this man in the face of an almost insuperable physical obstacle testifies to his involvement with life. In 1952 George developed detached retinas and went completely blind. This stopped him not one solitary whit. He has kept going, and is presently writing and lecturing—doing many things sighted people would love to do if they had the gift.

Then there is George's younger brother, Bill Torporcer, who of course also shared those early days on the East Side of New York. Somewhere along the line Bill heard of my interest in verse, and recently he sent some remarkable poetry. In one of his sonnets Bill re-creates a picture he and I wondered at all those years ago—the picture of beauty seeking to maintain itself in the midst of turbulent squalor.

As a kid, I was constantly amazed at a place on Second Avenue where the elevated train turned into Twenty-third Street and went south, then west again, and down through the narrow confines of Allen Street. How they managed to get that el structure between those tortuously close buildings I'll never know. I used to marvel at it as I went to work each morning. I'd stand there, looking at that ingenious workmanship, almost waiting for the train to plow into one of those corner buildings. And in those corner buildings, dingy, heavy, and stolid, one could see even further evidences of man's ability to reach up out of his confinement. Bill Torporcer put all of this into a sonnet:

30. . . . at the oars . . .

31. & 32. . . . with some friends . . .

33. . . . and on the trotting track.

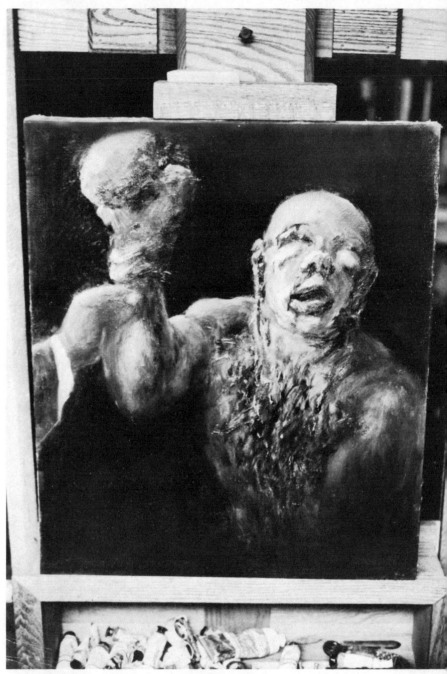

34. *The Victor*—"chronic progressive fibrotic encephalopathy" (punch drunk). Oil portrait by Cagney.

PLANTS ON THE FIRE ESCAPES OF THE SLUMS

Amidst the ragged and the underfed
The love of beauty raises up its head
In this poor quarter. Existence struggles
For its daily needs, yet wants, finds time to
Nourish some few seeds with sun and water.
Here potted red geraniums meet the eye
On bits of string, pale morning glories rise
In grotesque bow'rs with squalid poverty
Around begirt. What moves man's heart to grant
A plot of dirt the boon of flowers I
Know not. Yet I know to beauty's door the
Polished wealthy and the ragged poor both
Come a-knocking. One builds a garden on
His acres wide; the other in a single
Bloom takes pride—each heart unlocking.

Now, I submit this is one hell of a job of poetry. And when one remembers that it was written over fifty years ago when Bill was a kid, the achievement looms even higher. From first to last, it bespeaks life involvement and that wonderful gift that comes free to us all if we will only take it—and with which life is enriched beyond description—wonder.

Some fifty years ago, I can vividly remember sitting beside a newly cut tree stump while the sun was streaming down on it, catching the almost invisible motes dancing and bouncing in the air. Suddenly I noticed a little spider leaping up, grabbing something I couldn't see, and dropping back on the stump to eat its prey. All I could see was the sun and the dust motes, but that spider was worrying away at its meal, doubtless feeling a sense of genuine accomplishment. Pondering that little episode made me realize once again that many, many things exist in life that we don't see, hear, or understand—to our loss. I put it this way:

All space is filled with wondrous things,
Unseen by human eye.

Before us hover queens and kings,
With realms that float and fly.
It was wise of them to make a choice,
And decide to remain invisible,
For early in the game they found,
To be seen is to be divisible.
Finding the world is full of hate,
Afflicting alike the small, the great,
Knowing no bounds, or social stations,
Enveloping towns, destroying nations,
Refusing all manner of Christian teaching,
Laughing aloud at the earnest beseeching
Of thoughtful men in thankless jobs;
Cynically calling them deluded slobs,
For presuming to hold that The Christ is living,
And all that's good is of God's own giving.

❧ 13 ❧

If these pages are to be at least adequately self-revealing, it would seem essential that I talk a bit about my political coloration. That, after all, is—or should be—a vital part of a person's care and concern for the society in which he lives. I have tried through the years to maintain an active interest in the forces and influences that control our country.

When I was a young guy in the early 1920s, I met a man who was a Socialist. He had a place out in Free Acres, New Jersey, where he was constructing a cabin for an artist friend. At this time the vaudeville act my Bill and I were working was in trouble, bookings were scarce indeed, and so I was most pleased when my Socialist friend, knowing our bad situation, kindly asked me if I wanted to go out to the country and help him with the cabin. With the ever-present necessity of keeping alive I accepted unhesitatingly.

Free Acres at the time was a single-tax colony. Every conceivable kind of political philosophy was represented there. There were Communists, although nobody thought of them as Communists at the time; they were essentially Socialists. Then there were the philosophical anarchists, and the Republicans, and, of course, the Democrats. These people had acquired a quarter-acre of land, put up a little house, and made that their home base. When I got there at twenty-one years of age, I had no fixed political philosophy. I hadn't any idea of anything really. My big concern of the moment was where the next meal was coming from. It was only with the passing of time that I found out that the man who had invited me, Will Crawford, was a Socialist, as were many of his friends.

It would be odd indeed, given my age and sense of gratitude, if I hadn't imbibed some of their philosophy. This was never in any doctrinaire fashion. It was just a question of my lending a voice to the protests of the very troublesome times of the twenties. Then, with the passing of the years, I began to see the fallacies of any kind of doctrinaire approach. Increasingly, in my book, to take a hard-and-fast approach was a great mistake. As my life interests grew, I assumed what might in general be called a liberal stance.

In the 1940s, a defense fund was created to raise legal fees to free Tom Mooney, who had been implicated in the Preparedness Day parade bombing of 1916. I had read an awful lot about Mooney's situation and became very interested in it. The material I read was insistent in its position that Mooney and his cohort, Warren K. Billings, had been framed by the district attorney of San Francisco. I was invited to go up to San Francisco to help Mr. Mooney, and I actually went into the prison. I wasn't allowed to talk to him, but I waved to him and he waved to me.

After leaving the prison, we went to a meeting at some big hall there whose name eludes me, but I have never in my life seen such a wild-eyed gang as that group. They were absolutely nuts.

Screaming, yelling, giving vent to God knows what psychotic upsets, and doing everything except what one would consider appropriate to helping their man in prison. That was the end of that for me. I never went back. There is also the time when a collection was taken up around Hollywood to buy an ambulance for the Spanish Republican Army. As a soft touch, I contributed, and that was all you had to do those days to get yourself in a very unhappy position. The public was convinced that anybody who gave a dollar to the government forces in Spain was a wild-eyed Communist. My liberal "reputation" grew.

Subsequently I got involved in a liberal group, the name of which I have mercifully forgotten. It had a leftist slant, was very well organized, and made a point of recruiting celebrities, among them Ronald Reagan and myself. When Ronnie and I saw in which direction the group was headed, we both resigned the same night. From that time forth neither of us looked back to where we'd been.

I had worked for Mr. Roosevelt in his early campaigns, and I was still for him in 1940 when Willkie ran for the presidency. My close pal Bob Montgomery was a Willkie man, and this of course made not the slightest difference to our friendship. In the American system, differences of opinion were not only allowed, they were cultivated, not as so frequently in these days thrust stark and unmannerly at you. So Bob gave a big party on election night, installing a ticker tape in his home, invited some old Republican friends—and the Cagneys. I said to Bob, "I think you're making a mistake inviting me and my Bill. We'll be like the death head at the feast."

"Well," said Bob, "if you don't come, I won't give the party."

We went. It was black-tie, all very fancy. My wife wore a huge Roosevelt button, and when we walked into this group of rabid Republicans, we were received in some quarters with coolness. Old Frank Craven, with whom I'd just finished a picture, wouldn't even shake hands with me. In any case, my Bill was wearing a low-cut dress with her Roosevelt button very forthrightly displayed on her bosom, and one Republican said, "Well, where she wears it, you can't hate it." That was one of the very few laughs of the evening. When the result of the ticker tape began chattering away, even the few laughs remaining dwindled away to silence.

As a decidedly Rooseveltian Democrat, actors of conservative kidney at that time looked on me with scant warmth. John Wayne didn't like me at all, and I didn't approve of him because I thought he was being used by Louis B. Mayer and the rest of the producers to set up what I called a company union in opposition to the Screen Actors Guild. John's union was quite conservative, but I never thought of it in that way; I could only see its being used by the producers. John couldn't see my point of view at all, and I don't blame him for that. Now, with the passing of time, my strong conservatism has placed me generally in John's camp. A remarkable man, John. When one realizes he has played virtually the same part over the years, wearing virtually the same clothing, and maintaining a very high status in the business, it's clear that whatever John Wayne is, people love him, and that's about the best recommendation I can think of. His staunch patriotism and concern for his country's welfare are frequently derided by the liberal left, and they try to laugh at him. But nobody laughs at John Wayne. He can make himself felt wherever he is and whatever he does.

My move to conservatism was precipitated by my lack of admiration for Mr. Truman's performance after he took over from FDR, and so I cast my first non-Democratic vote, for Tom Dewey. When Dewey was defeated, I called Bob Montgomery and said, "Well, I took care of your boy, didn't I? I cast my first Republican vote and down he goes."

In my liberal days I was helped to remain that way on at least one occasion by a negative studio stimulus. In 1934 the studio heads took it upon themselves to defeat a California gubernatorial candidate, Upton Sinclair. Sinclair had been a propagandist for the left all his creative life, and as a Socialist had written some

wonderfully enlightening books on the horrors that came out of
the Chicago packing houses, and similar social evils. The studio
heads decided that the way to defeat Sinclair was to collect two
days' pay from all employees and donate this "contribution" to
Sinclair's opponent. I refused, and at a meeting held at the studio,
Jack Warner said, "There's a guy in the studio who one of these
days is gonna need a favor from us. And will he get it? No. Because he's a professional against-er." I rather got the idea he
meant me, but I cared not at all. Let's say that I disagreed with
thinking that made these studio heads sound and act like feudal
lords.

In any case, I believe in my bones that my going from the liberal stance to the conservative was a totally natural reaction once
I began to see the undisciplined elements in our country stimulating a breakdown of our system. From what I've seen of the liberal
attitudes toward the young and the permissive attitudes in the
schools, and everybody pulling every which way from center, I
consider these all inimical to the health of our nation. Those func-
tionless creatures, the hippies, for example, just didn't appear out
of a vacuum. A few words came to me one day about their curious
lethargy:

> Disturb not their fixed, eternal placidity,
> Don't delay their rambling rush to nowhere,
> Their need for nothing, non-requires validity.
> Their boat is a void demanding they go where
> Nothing's a must and nothing's a rule,
> Just to live and breathe and stare and stool.

To repeat, people like this just don't happen. I blame much of
our problems with today's youth on the liberal boys, the gang
with no fixed view of things, no absolutes. Like the shifting sands,
they accommodate to any passing cloud of fancy—to whatever
they think is best for them at the moment. By implication they
say: do anything you damned well like.

But conceivably, sadly, maybe Clemenceau, the old Tiger of

France, was right when he said, "The affairs of men are so complicated that rather than try to solve them, it's better to let them kill each other." I think it was also Clemenceau who said, "I wouldn't give a sou for any young man who hadn't been a Socialist by the time he was twenty—but I would be perfectly willing to kick his behind if he were still a Socialist by the time he was forty." I escaped Clemenceau's wrath on both counts, and I can now consider myself an archconservative.

When one looks at the Watergate business, it is disheartening to see exposed the behavior of people in high places, drawing fabulous salaries supposedly in the service of their country, when it is really themselves that they are serving. It's shocking. I got a letter from a lady recently in which she said, "I'm sixty-five and I have all the apprehensions of the aged person. Where does our country stand now? Are we tobogganing toward destruction?" That and other misgivings she sounded in a really fine letter. I answered, "Dear Mrs. So-and-So: Do be of some cheer. Early on in my life I read a book that contained the sayings of famous men on their deathbed. One of the most striking comments was the Duke of Wellington's. He said in effect that he was glad he was dying because the world was going up in flames to utter destruction and he didn't want to be around to see that. Scant consolation, perhaps, in that—but the Iron Duke uttered those words in 1852, and the world is still around."

The Watergate business is simply an extension of this monumental kind of self-seeking that debauches our leadership. And this general scheme is going on right now in Peking and Moscow and Addis Ababa. Everywhere is that fella with the aim that he is going to be somebody at anybody's cost. Anybody's cost except his own, of course. These men because of their strong ambitions get the good jobs, and when they get close to the seat of power, they think they can do no wrong. They use that power for their own purposes and are above penalty. I must say I was physically ill at the entire picture of Watergate. Now that Mr. Nixon has been found wanting, will it rest there? We mustn't forget that there are forces in America that do not want Mr. Nixon, Mr. Ford, or any other kind of conservative or near conservative in office, and these forces are bent on finding power, too.

Bob Montgomery sent me a press cutting a short time ago. It's an editorial treating of England in 1783, and its description of the British political turmoils of that year sounds exactly like our current situation: corruption rampant, the country almost bankrupt, a pervasive loss of faith in leadership. Then along came William Pitt the Younger, who threw his great strength into the chaos and reversed the downward order of things. Why are we today in the same difficulty as the English then? I think it's all grounded in one thing: lack of integrity. The only thing we can do is hope things will reverse themselves, but it's going to take a very strong character to walk in and say, "Ladies and gentlemen, it's not working at the moment, is it? Let's do something about it!" Someone has to move the country at whatever sacrifice to himself. Which is what FDR did when he got in office—changed the whole country around. Business said he was great until he started to step on business's toes—and we're still feeling the results of that kind of thing.

One great American leader was a particular hero of mine: Teddy Roosevelt, that wonderful maverick. Tom Platt, the Republican senator and head of the Republican party in New York in the nineties, just couldn't figure Teddy out. Tom, having played by his own rules and the rules of the political game of his time, just couldn't understand Teddy doing the things he did or saying the things he said. "He's a *nut!*" Tom said about Teddy. "But you know something else? He's going to be elected!" And he was—with Tom Platt's forceful help.

I was approached to play Teddy about fifteen years ago, and I would have been glad to do so if a script with some depth had been available. But none was.

In these sad days, our country could use another Pitt the Younger or Teddy Roosevelt to move us, to get us going again.

But at least let's be thankful for what we have in the way of liberties and safeguards. Imagine what would happen in a more authoritative government when the ambitious few find themselves in positions of authority! It's the old story of the ambitious few trying to rule the many, as now obtains in Russia. Years ago I knew Lincoln Steffens, the great muckraker, and as an enthusiastic Socialist, one remark of his is remembered perhaps more than any of his others. After a trip to Russia, he said, "I have seen the future and it works." I often wonder what Steffens, as a professional author, would think of Russia today and its treatment of Boris Pasternak, Alexander Solzhenitsyn, and the Soviet Jews.

It's manifest to me that one's point of view is the essential clue to one's life function. A good friend of mine, a reliably solid actor who'd been around many a year, said to me one day that he'd be scared to play the lead in a picture. "I'd be frightened by it," he said. I asked him why and he said he didn't relish the responsibility of it. "Didn't that ever occur to you?" he asked. I could honestly say it never had because all I thought about was not the position or my aptitude or anything else. To me this was just a job to be done, and I did it to the best of my ability. It never occurred to me to shirk the job just because I was afraid of it. This touches on the Watergate business in that if a reliable young person isn't willing to enter the halls of government and take on the needed responsibility for the betterment of us all, an *un*reliable young person can easily come along and do the job to the detriment of us all.

Politics needs more than ever these days young people of remarkable talent—incipient Lincolns—who can help refurbish this old world. A long time ago I wrote a little something that touches on those who can help us to a better existence:

> The function, soul, of genius,
> Is to renovate the new,
> And open doors to vistas
> Hitherto unseen or even partly known,
> So that those who follow after
> Can make some part, however small, their own.

⤳ 14 ⤳

The last curtain call is usually the nicest. When it's time to go, you should go. I've always thought how sad it is to see fellas and gals hanging on and hanging on after the party is over and the applause has died. It's sad because if there is any one truth about show business, it's that the finish is written before the prologue. Inevitably, after the career has had its ups and downs—and some of those ups can be breathlessly high—there comes a time when the jig is up, and when it's up in show business, my dear fella, it's up.

I've seen the biggest of them who just could not understand what had happened when the time came and they had to make their exits. One chap I know has never recovered. In his bitterness he says he's just as good as ever and just as big as ever in the minds of the people. Nothing can unsell him on the idea that he's still a top-flight star. Alas, he isn't.

So, in my retirement, I have steadfastly refused to come back, until just recently, and that was only a one-night stand. It was a last bow I was induced to make by reason of a strong cultural need. Movies have been around just a comparatively short time, really, in terms of all the other art forms. When you consider the fact that the theatre is over two thousand years old and that movies were first presented commercially in New York just four years before I was born, the contrast in longevity is startling.

Yet movies are undoubtedly the most potent art form of our day, and despite some of the miserable slop that is being dished out these days, the film is still a great force and will undoubtedly go from strength to strength. It's astonishing that in the film's comparatively short life so very, very many movies were made. One reliable historian estimates that there were a quarter million of them across the world, which is no small number. Naturally, most of those were programmers, good for giving the pleasures of the day, and little more. But a surprisingly large number of these pictures were works of art, or close thereto. Another not inconsiderable proportion of these films tell the story of their time so vividly that they bear out most accurately Shakespeare's assertion that the players are the abstract and brief chronicles of the time.

The American Film Institute was founded to preserve the great heritage of our films, many of which have just been thrown away after their brief runs as just so much wastepaper. Both in order to preserve vital films of our past and also to encourage young people to become creative film-makers, the AFI, like any other new and growing cultural institution, needs ample funding.

Candidly, I have never given a damn about awards, but when the AFI suggested that I receive their 1974 Life Achievement Award, I realized they weren't doing it all altruistically, and understandably so. They have a need for some person to hang this yearly fund-raising event on, and without the yearly event they would have a very rough time of it financially. I was happy to be of some use.

In preparing for the banquet on March 13, 1974, when I was to get the award, I was asked to help publicize the affair in the weeks just prior to it. For a guy who had hoped that a happy anonymity was to be his permanent lot in life, this was quite some doing, but of course I was determined that once I had made the decision, I would do the job all the way. So it was that I welcomed the guys and gals of the press on several occasions, and I took ample care to sell the AFI message. One day during this period while waiting for the *TV Guide* photographer to come over, it occurred to me that if anybody had forecast such a thing a year ago I would have told them they were perilously close to mental dysfunction.

The evening was thoroughly satisfactory, seeing old friends, watching clips from the old films, and it gave me and mine a great feeling of warmth and pleasure. How could it be otherwise when one heard such kind words from people like John Wayne, Bob Hope, Doris Day, Mae Clarke, Cicely Tyson, George C. Scott, Frank Gorshin (who sang and danced an imitation of me with

Kirk Douglas and George Segal), Ronnie Reagan, Frank Sinatra
(who emceed beautifully and sang me a song in the same style),
Shirley MacLaine, and Jack Lemmon?

One of the really amusing things of the evening was furnished by my little niece, Terry, and my sister Jeanne. Terry
said to Jeannie, "Now, Mom, you've got to understand something.
This is one evening you are not supposed to cry." The source of
that remark is that every time I do a dance routine, Jeannie starts
to cry, and Terry was emphasizing that tonight it wasn't to be
done. So came the moment when they flashed on the screen the
tabletop routine with Bob Hope from *The Seven Little Foys*.
Jeannie, remembering her daughter's admonishment, looked over
at her—and there was Terry watching it, gulping, the tears running down her cheeks. Then Jeannie, of course, gave way too,
but not visibly.

By the time I got up to speak, I must admit to a certain ex-
penditure of nerves. This is part of what I said:

"I'm a wreck. You know, when my friend A. C. Lyles told me
of the plans that the AFI had for this evening, it gave me pause.
And I said to him, 'You know, this is not the kind of thing I do
every day. What will they expect of me?' And he said, 'Oh, well,
all you have to do is "Uhm uhh uhm." ' And I said, 'What's that?'
He said, 'All you have to do is "Uhm uhh uhm." ' So I'm saying to
you right now with a little necessary emphasis, 'Mmhm, mhmm,
mhmm.'

"And about the award, I'm very grateful for it. But why don't
we just say for now that I'm merely the custodian, holding it for
all those wonderful guys and gals who worked over the years to
bring about this night for me? I really mean it. I'm thanking you
for them and for me.

"Young George Stevens in a letter to me early on told me that
one of the fundamental aims of the AFI was to establish it firmly
as an art form. Art. Now, I'm a little bit hipped on the thing
myself and have been for a long time. And it brought to mind a
work written by John Masefield, the English poet laureate. He

wrote it with a pen dipped in a bit of vitriol. I'm going to read it to you now.

> What is the hardest task of art?
> To clear the ground and make a start
> 'Midst wooden head and iron heart;
> To sing the stopp'd adder's ear
> To fill the tale with none to hear,
> And paint what none else reckon dear;
> To dance or carve or build or strive
> Among the dead or half alive
> Whom greeds impel and terrors drive.
> Now you, my English dancers, you
> Began our English joy anew
> In sand with neither rain nor dew,
> Dance with despised and held in shame
> Almost something not to name
> But that lovely flower came.
> Oh, may you prosper till the race
> Is all one rapture at your grace,
> And England beauty's dwelling place.
> Then you'll know what Shakespeare knew
> That when the millions want the few
> They can make heaven here—and do.

"I like that.

"I have a great many thanks to spread about this evening. We all know an event like this doesn't get itself on. It is the result of a lot of dedicated people working at peak pitch for a great many days.

"So, Frankie—Frankie Sinatra—one of the neighbors' children. Thanks for the song. How many copies it will sell, uhm uhh uhm. And Ted Ashley, George Stevens, Sue Taurog, Chuck Heston, Mr. Scott, dear Doris Day, Bob Hope, Shirley MacLaine, Jack Lemmon, Miss Tyson, Frank Gorshin—oh, Frankie, just in passing: I never said, 'Mmm, you dirty rat!' What I actually did say was 'Judy! Judy! Judy!' And thank you, Mr. Segal, big Duke

Wayne, blessing—and Kirk Douglas. Oh, and one more thing, Frankie Gorshin, that hitching of the trousers, I got that from a fella who hung out on the corner of Seventy-eighth Street and First Avenue. I was about twelve years old and he was most interesting to me because that's all he did [*the gesture*] all day. When somebody would greet him, he didn't deign to say hello, he just stood back and did this: [*the greeting twitch*]. Now, let's face it. We are all indebted to that fella. He was a type—and we had them. Oh, how we did have them. . . .

"And the names, the names, the names of my youth. Lagerhead Quinlavan. Artie Klein. Pete Leyden. Jake Brodkin. Specs Torporcer. Brother O'Meara. Picky Houlihan. Were all part of a stimulating early environment which produced that unmistakable touch of the gutter without which this evening might never have happened at all."

And that was the end of a wonderful evening.

Everything went along beautifully, and as far as I could tell, I made only one slipup—the great number of people I didn't mention. In retrospect, what I should have said was that—inasmuch as there were so many people who were such a vital part of my thirty years in the business—mentioning a few would be a mistake. What I did instead was to try to mention quite a few. I worked hard at it, and I had a large number of names at hand. I had this big list of people on the back of one of the shirt cards on which I had written my speech. I had intended to use my reading glasses when speaking, but I was asked not to. I don't care one tinker's damn if anybody sees me in glasses or not, but I was asked to refrain, and since I wasn't running the show, I did what was required. As a result I had to print my speech in large block letters on the shirt boards with a black-felt pen. In flipping these over at appropriate points, I misflipped—and I "lost" one whole side, and with it a bunch of names I very much wanted to cite.

But everybody in my working life knows who they are, I trust—and to them I am deeply, deeply grateful, because this is one business where the phrase "no man is an island" is so strongly applicable. There are some people in pictures who thought they had done it all by themselves, and as I look back at such people, they seem to me so very sad. Motion pictures always were, and still very much are, a collaborative enterprise.

CBS telecast the banquet a few days later to an audience of close to fifty million, they tell me, and gratifyingly the response to Charlton Heston's appeal over the air for AFI contributions was fulsome. Nearly forty-five thousand dollars in contributions to support the institute's educational and historical programs came in. There's nothing as nice as a *rewarding* happy ending.

Not long after the AFI proceedings and as a pleasant after-piece to it, Jack Lemmon came over to visit, and he told us a story that I can't forbear giving—not because of the subject matter certainly, but because it's so wittily, typically Jack. He is the only one qualified to tell it.

JACK LEMMON:

"I had a meeting here in Los Angeles with Jason Miller one day. He was sort of fresh from New York, having done only two pictures and still living back East. So he was kind of getting his feet wet in California. At the time of our meeting he was deeply engrossed in the casting of the film to be made from his play *The Championship Season*. We met at the Hideaway Bar of the Beverly Wilshire Hotel. As we sat at the bar itself, we did the 'Hi!,' 'How are you?' routine, and commenced chatting.

"We had been talking no more than two minutes when suddenly he turned to me with a topic that was clearly predominant in his mind. 'You know,' he said, 'this casting business has been driving me crazy, but I've got one obsession about it. What do you think of Jimmy Cagney?'

"I turned to him and said, 'What do I think of Jimmy Cagney?' And at that point—*precisely* at *that* moment—there was an earthquake tremor.

"It was a ripper. Perhaps a three or a four on the Richter scale. The bar shook, the ashtrays bounced around, the drinks were sloshing, the chandeliers were swaying. I knew exactly what it was. Also, somewhere in the back of my mind that little light bulb went on, and I realized what a dramatic moment this was.

"So I just kept staring straight at him. I didn't swerve, didn't move a muscle. Jason grabbed the bar. Panic set in his eyes, he stared straight ahead. Then as the earthquake stopped just a very few seconds later, he turned and looked at me.

"And I said very seriously and quickly, 'That's what I think of Jimmy Cagney!'"

I think that's an utterly charming story.

So—after all the interviews and the great evening itself, the American Film Institute event is set firmly in my mind as one of the pleasantest memories of my life, and I now go back to irrevocable retirement in pleasant fettle.

There have been some interesting attempts in recent years to get me out of retirement. I was tempted only once. When George Cukor was preparing for the film of *My Fair Lady*, he called Katie Hepburn to make a connection, and she obliged, calling me to ask if it was all right to give Cukor my phone number. Agreed. He called, offering me the role of Doolittle, a great part if there ever was one, in a great show with great numbers. I must say that although I'd been out of the business five or six years with no thought at all of returning, for a brief moment I thought—maybe. Maybe I'd like to do this last one. *My Fair Lady* has so much richness, everything about it is so fine.

But then I told George, "Oh, what the hell, I've committed myself to retirement and I've down deep no interest in going back." He wouldn't take no for an answer and I gently tried to discourage him, but he wouldn't stay discouraged. He said to hold off making a decision at least until I had returned to California (I was then East). When I got back, I called him.

"George, I want to save you the ignominy of calling the actor again."

"Will you do it?"

"George, no."

"Oh, goddamn, Jim, come on. It would be such fun."

"Yeah, I suppose it would. But I just can't summon the interest. I really can't. The idea's attractive, the part would be a hell of a part, and exciting to do—all those wonderful numbers—but I think we'd better forget it."

So they went on without me, and that was fine, because Stanley Holloway is a wonderful entertainer, and he was great. That, then, is the only time I've ever had a slight tug to go back, and the tug was there only because I'm a song-and-dance man, and *My Fair Lady* was one hell of a song-and-dance picture.

Recently Francis Ford Coppola asked me to play a part in his *Godfather II*, but I told him I had no interest, that I wasn't coming out of retirement to do anything. Then, on his own, he flew his jet plane to see me at the farm. I picked him and his young son up at the airport and drove him out to the house. I think Mr. Coppola expected a mansion instead of my simple little stone house, and I suppose when I started to cook his breakfast (it was 7:00 A.M.), he may have wondered if it was the cook's day off. But my Bill and I are the only two cooks at our house, and the chief dishwashers too.

During breakfast and until about ten, Mr. Coppola and I chatted about the picture business, but we never got around to talking about *Godfather II*. Then I called Tom Fitzpatrick, the wonderful fella who cares for and supervises the breeding of the horses, and asked him to hitch up a pair for a drive through the woods. So away into the beautiful fall foliage we went, Mr. Coppola, his son, and I, for an hour or so. When we got back to the house, I said to the little fella, "Would you like to see some pretty horses?" He would, so down to the barn to see the lovely Morgans —horses that particularly appeal to youngsters because they are generally small animals with beautiful heads.

We spent almost an hour there, and then I said to Mr. Coppola, "Do you think you ought to be getting back to your plane?" He said he thought so. We got back into the car, and Tom drove us to the airport. Just before we got there, Mr. Coppola said, "Mr.

Cagney, I came here hoping to talk you out of retirement, to come and do this thing with us. But—what am I going to tell them that I haven't talked you out of retirement—you have talked me *into* it?" This was, of course, a very gracious thing to say, and a fine finish to our visit. I saw in this young man sterling talent and a humble, sensible point of view. I was glad I met him and I'm looking forward to the next time. But not behind a camera.

So I live my retirement busily every day, only getting really lazy, I must confess, once in a while at the Vineyard. Frank McHugh tells a classic story about me that he gave at a Pipe Night at The Players for Bob Montgomery, Frank, Rolie Winters, and me. Frank is a great observer and he was telling all assembled about his trip to visit me at the Vineyard.

As Frank tells it, I said to him, "Want to go down to the boat, Frank?" He said yes. We fixed lunch, got in the car, and drove down to the boat. We got out and walked leisurely down to the dock. We got in the boat, then I looked over the side into the water. Then I looked up at a flock of geese going by. Next, I looked over the side into the water again and observed a school of fishes. Then I shifted the lunch package from one arm to the other. Then I looked over at Lonesome Charlie the Cormorant sitting with his wings outspread, drying out on a mooring float. Next I looked at some ducks and gulls, then I looked down into the water again. I saw a bait trap, pulled it up, and said, "Well, I'm going to have to clean that out one of these days." Then I turned to Frank and said, "How about a nap?"

Frank killed them with that at The Players.

Some while ago I was asked by an eighty-six-year-old fella who in his youth had driven around in carriages just why I was so interested in them. I said, "Well, it seems to me that Chauncey and I have been trying to escape into the eighteenth century all our lives."

Chauncey, my neighbor and a horse and carriage devotee also, was standing with us. He corrected me quickly. "*Seventeenth* century," he said. And he was quite right. Not only were the times then less strenuous, but I think people were more innocent too. Today one can see an inordinate number of people who, in Bernard de Voto's phrase, suffer from an advanced case of ambition.

I've seen so many of them in the picture business. "Shrewd ignoramuses" I call them, and that's not a contradiction in terms. Truly shrewd, truly ignorant of the worthwhile; talentless people who prosper at the expense of the talented. Never really sure what their aims are, they can never truly be happy. They are totally amoral and ruthless and apparently don't give that a thought. After all, does a cancer realize it's a cancer? I wrote two lines about them:

These disciples of greed, born without fear, find no release from tension.
They spend their hours in a permanent state of miserable apprehension.

A part, are they, of what seems to be man's permanently inbuilt need to hurt?

In looking at my own flaws, I am duty bound to report that they have often been a source of irritation to me. One time, typically, I had mislaid something; indeed, I'd mislaid a number of things that morning, and I couldn't find *anything*. My own damned carelessness. I stopped dead finally, and standing in the middle of that room, thoroughly frustrated, I snapped through my clenched teeth, "My God, I'm sick and tired of being me."

But only under those conditions. Otherwise, it's been rewarding indeed, and now at seventy-six, one doesn't know the life expectancy, but the point is not to worry about it. Just assume everything is going to go on as is until whatever comes—and let it go at that.

I wrote a piece about an old man and a young woman who says to him:

Why do you weep, poor dear old man?
It hurts me within when you weep.

He answers:

> I weep for the long lost wonderful years
> I once thought were mine to keep.

She says:

> Why would you keep them, poor dear old man?
> That's too much to ask. Just living those so-called
> Wonderful years is life's most onerous task.
> For time passes and life passes and all
> Things end in the sadness,
> Except for those sometimes fortunate ones
> Who find peace in a benevolent madness.

Surely the vital thing in old age is to maintain an interest and never stop planning for the future. I started painting at sixty and am still intensely caught up in it. I am studying classical guitar and I've also just taken up the bugle, trying to learn all the traditional carriage calls. For my physical well-being, I still put on a record and do a chorus or two of buck dancing. It's a mistake to set limits on yourself; life will do that whether you like it or not. A successful life must be determined by one's attitude. In a favorite phrase of my brother Ed, "We live between our ears." Sermon over.

Recently I went to a party given by Sergei Bongart, my painting teacher—a most delightful affair with really interesting people—and, Bongart being Bongart, the best in the way of food prevailed. Prominent among the desserts were some napoleons that I can only describe as real works of art. Now, a napoleon to us as kids was a thing of awe and beauty—something never to be forgotten. My sister Jeannie was at the Bongarts' with me, and as we were going around the table, I pointed to one of these little masterpieces and said, "Honey, look—a napoleon!" We looked at each other and grinned. I said, "Let's take one to brother Bill." So Jeannie took it, wrapped it, and put it aside. The next day she gave it to Bill, and his joy at seeing this sumptuous thing was unbounded. He called me right away, and I asked him what he thought of it.

"Jim," he said, "I want to tell you I remember the first napoleon I ever had in my life. It was in Ridgewood. Mom brought some home—one for herself and one for each of her four boys. And that was an *event!*"

This little incident made me realize so clearly that, if in our childhood, we were given unlimited napoleons, we wouldn't have had the deep, deep pleasure it still gives us to sink a tooth into that superb pastry. Bill and I got to talking about a very rich man I know well who has never had a moment of deprivation in his life. To him a napoleon is just a napoleon; to us it was, it *is*, an experience. It points up that in the early days of our family, no matter how tough things were, and God knows they were tough, we still feel we had the best of it because we knew how to enjoy things when we got them.

A friend wrote this to me a bit ago about the far-away fella business: "Yes, I'd say Pat gave you the right designation. You're a far-away fella in any number of ways. As a kid you used to look at other people and say to yourself, 'I wonder what it would be like to be them?,' and so you grew up to be a man with the gift of wonder, which allows you to observe people and places analytically. You became a man out of the common run of activity who loves the solitudes and the elements—a non-city man from the city. You're a man with the reputation of being a semi-recluse when actually—and here's the drama of the thing—you're more involved with living than the vast majority in the churning bowels of the city. In all these ways and more, you were born and you will die a far-away fella."

If the foregoing is true, and I'd like to think it is, it has come about through things I had very little to do with. My parents were a gift, and so was my family; I was lucky enough to marry the girl I did, and have the children I did; my good friends came to me unbidden; my job was one I enjoyed; and I've lived my life trying to be true to all these.

Which is my story to date. So, in Jim Barton's words, thanks for the use of the hall. Thanks, too, for buying the tickets that

gave me this lovely and deeply loved farm whence these words
come. And, above all, the very number of those tickets prompt me
to say: grateful thanks for giving a song-and-dance man across
the years all those heart-warming encores.